Rand McNally
PICTURE ATLAS
OF THE WORLD

Illustrated by Brian Delf

✦ Rand McNally

Chicago · New York · San Francisco

Rand McNally
The Picture Atlas of the World

1993 revised edition published by
Rand McNally in the U.S.A

First published in Great Britain in 1991
by Dorling Kindersley Limited,
9 Henrietta Street, London WC2E 8PS
Reprinted with revisions 1991
Second edition 1992
Reprinted with revisions 1993

Text by Richard Kemp

Art Editor Lester Cheeseman
Designer Marcus James
Project Editor Susan Peach
Senior Editor Emma Johnson
Consultant Keith Lye
Production Teresa Solomon
Art Director Roger Priddy

Reproduced in Hong Kong by Bright Arts
Printed and bound in Italy by New Interlitho, Milan

Library of Congress Cataloging-in-Publication Data

Picture atlas of the world / illustrated by Brian Delf. – 1993 rev. ed.
   p. cm.
   At head of title: Rand McNally.
   Includes index.
   Summary: Maps of the different regions of the world
show their geographic, cultural, and economic features.
Includes text describing the individual countries.
   ISBN 0-528-83564-5
   1. Atlases. [1. Atlases. 2. Geography.] I. Delf, Brian, ill.
II. Rand McNally and Company. III. Title: Rand McNally
picture atlas of the world.
G1021.P65 1993 <G&M>
912--dc20
                                    92-37056
                                         CIP
                                    MAP AC

CONTENTS

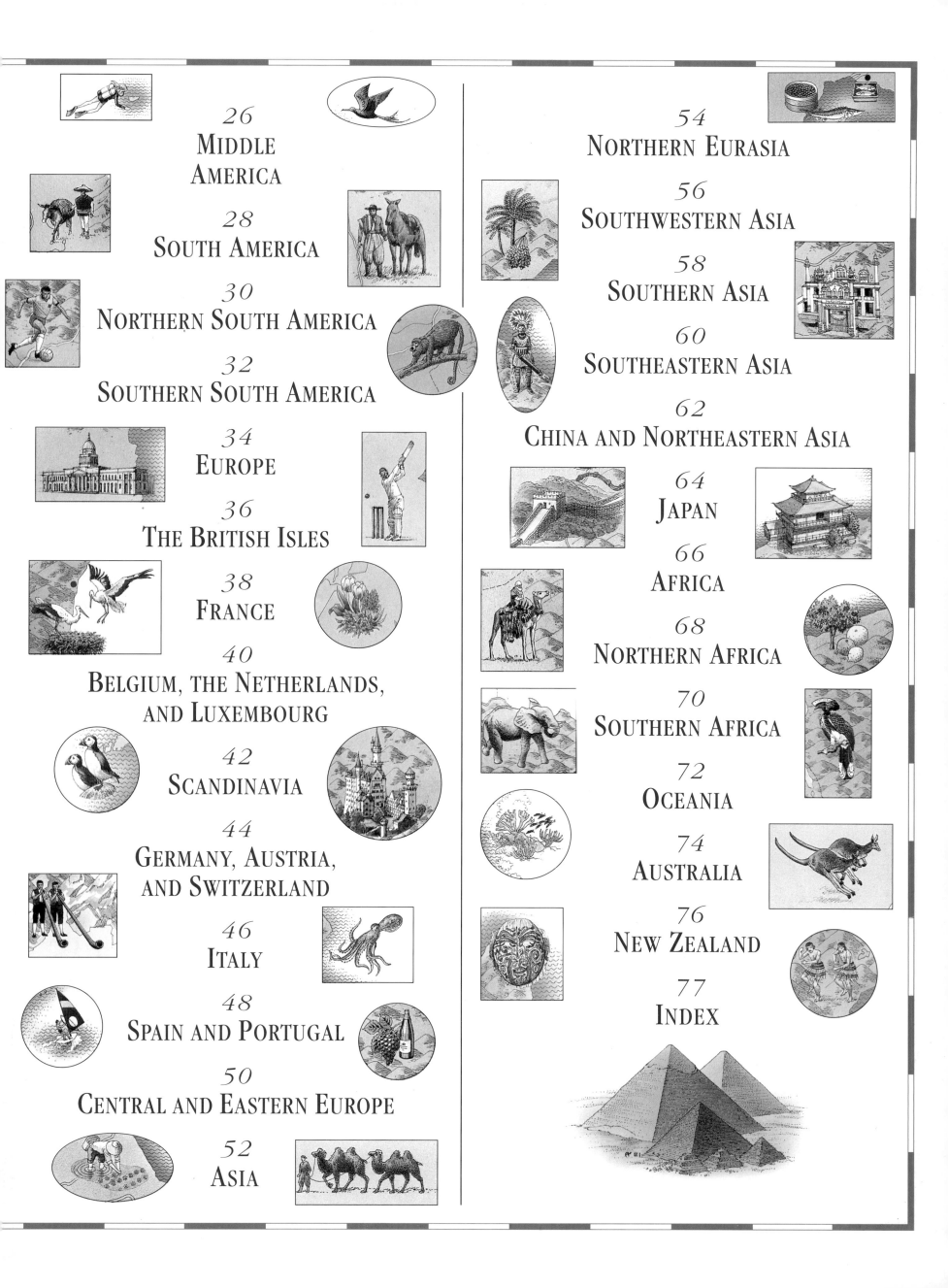

OUR PLANET EARTH

THE EARTH on which we live is one of a family of nine planets which circle around a star called the sun. The sun is just one of about 100 billion stars in our galaxy. On a clear night you can see some of the other stars in the galaxy as a glow in the sky, called the milky way. Astronomers estimate that there may be as many as 10 billion galaxies, which together make up the universe.

THE SOLAR SYSTEM

The sun is much bigger than the planets. It has a diameter of about 864,948 miles (1,392,000 km). The diameter of the earth at the equator is only 7,747 miles (12,714 km).

The distance from the sun to the earth is about 93 million miles (150 million km). If a train left earth at a speed of 110 mph (175 kph), it would take 96 years to reach the sun.

THE EARTH'S SHIELD

The earth is like a giant magnet. It has two magnetic poles, which lie near the north and south poles. The earth's magnetism is probably caused by movement of the molten metals in its outer core. Around the earth is a region called the magnetosphere, which acts as a huge shield. It protects the earth from the solar wind, a stream of electrically charged particles from the sun. Particles that get through the magnetosphere are trapped in the Van Allen belts.

THE SEASONS AND DAYS

It takes a year for the earth to circle the sun. The earth is slightly tilted, so one half of the globe, or hemisphere, is closer to the sun than the other. This tilt causes the seasons. The hemisphere tilted towards the sun receives more heat, and so has summer, while the hemisphere that is tilted away has winter. As it circles the sun, the earth also spins on its axis, turning once every 24 hours. This rotation causes our days and nights. The side of the earth facing the sun has day, while the other side has night.

MARCH
Spring in the northern hemisphere.

DECEMBER
Summer in the southern hemisphere.

MOON

SUN

JUNE
Summer in the northern hemisphere.

SEPTEMBER
Spring in the southern hemisphere.

THE ATMOSPHERE

The atmosphere is a layer of gases surrounding the earth. It is about 621 miles (1,000 km) thick and is made of nitrogen, oxygen, carbon dioxide, water vapor, and small amounts of other gases. The atmosphere acts as a protective shield, absorbing much of the heat that reaches the earth from the sun. Without it, our whole planet would be burnt to a desert.

Most of the gases in the atmosphere are concentrated in the lowest part, which is called the troposphere. Above this is the stratosphere. This contains the ozone layer, which absorbs harmful ultraviolet rays from the sun. Above the stratosphere are the mesosphere and the thermosphere. Here the gases are so thin that there is little difference between these parts of the atmosphere and space.

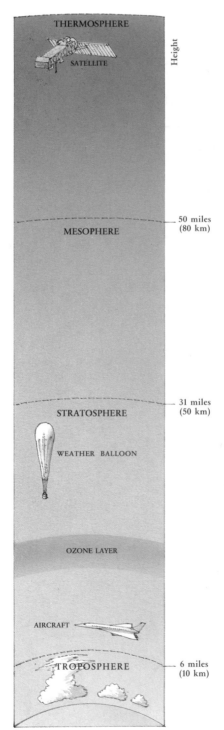

THERMOSPHERE

SATELLITE

Height

MESOSPHERE

50 miles (80 km)

STRATOSPHERE

31 miles (50 km)

WEATHER BALLOON

OZONE LAYER

AIRCRAFT

TROPOSPHERE

6 miles (10 km)

INSIDE THE EARTH

Scientists believe that the earth was formed about 4.6 billion years ago from a spinning cloud of gas and dust, which shrank to form a hot ball of liquid, or molten, rock. As it cooled, the earth's surface formed into a solid crust. Under the surface the temperature is so high that parts of the earth are still liquid. Movement of this molten material in the outer core is thought to produce the earth's magnetic fields.

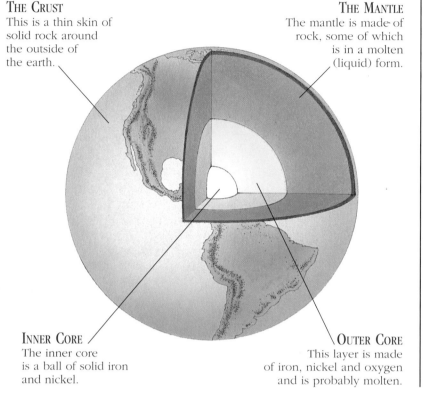

THE CRUST
This is a thin skin of solid rock around the outside of the earth.

THE MANTLE
The mantle is made of rock, some of which is in a molten (liquid) form.

INNER CORE
The inner core is a ball of solid iron and nickel.

OUTER CORE
This layer is made of iron, nickel and oxygen and is probably molten.

THE WANDERING CONTINENTS

The earth's crust is made up of pieces called plates, which float on top of a layer of molten rock in the mantle. There are seven main plates and several smaller ones. The magnetic forces within the earth move the plates slowly around the globe in an ever-changing jigsaw.

Geologists believe that about 270 million years ago all the land on earth was joined together in one "super-continent," which they call Pangaea. But, as the plates moved around, the land in this super-continent, slowly started to split up. This movement is called continental drift. The maps below show how geologists think the continents have moved and split apart to form the landmasses that we know today.

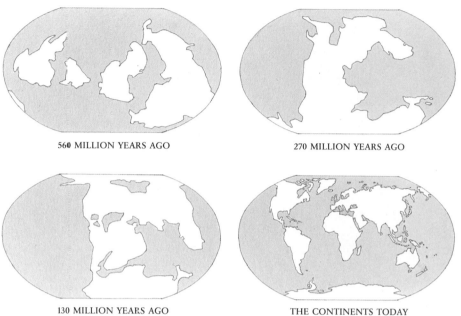

560 MILLION YEARS AGO

270 MILLION YEARS AGO

130 MILLION YEARS AGO

THE CONTINENTS TODAY

THE RESTLESS EARTH

As the plates move around the globe they collide, overlap, and slide past each other. The plates travel very slowly – their fastest speed is about 6 in (15 cm) in a year – but over millions of years the results of this movement can be dramatic. Huge mountain ranges, spectacular rift valleys, and deep trenches in the ocean bed have all been formed in areas where two plates meet. Earthquakes, volcanoes, geysers and hot mud pools are also caused by plate movements. The regions in the world where they are found closely follow the joins between the plates.

SLIDING PAST
The San Andreas Fault in California is an example of a place where two plates are sliding past each other. The sliding movement often occurs in short bursts which are felt on the surface as earthquakes.

GOING UNDER
If two plates collide, the edge of one can be forced under the other into the mantle below, forming a deep ocean trench. The rocks from the crust melt in the mantle. Often these molten rocks force their way to the surface to form volcanoes.

PULLING APART
When two plates pull apart, molten rocks from the mantle come up to fill the gap. If this happens on the ocean floor it creates underwater mountain ridges. On land, it forms steep-sided valleys, such as the Great Rift Valley in East Africa.

COLLISION COURSE
Sometimes when two plates collide rocks are forced up to form great mountain ranges. These mountains are often volcanic. The Andes range in South America and the Himalayas in Asia were both formed by colliding plates.

CLIMATES AROUND THE WORLD

CLIMATE is the name given to the typical weather conditions and temperature in a particular area. Similar types of climate are found in different places around the world. For example, there are regions of hot, dry desert in Africa, North America, and central Australia.

The climate in any particular place depends partly on its latitude, that is, how far north or south of the equator it lies. The regions around the equator are the hottest places in the world. The further away from the equator you go, the colder the climate becomes. The coldest places in the world are the polar regions around the north and south poles.

Climate is also affected by how close a place is to the sea. The sea warms and cools the land near it, so coastal areas usually have fewer extremes of temperature than places in the center of a continent. Another important influence is altitude – how high a place is above sea level. The higher the place, the colder is its climate.

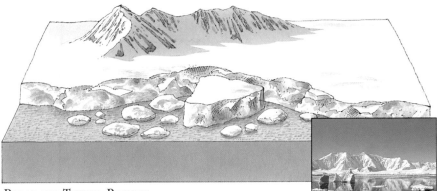

POLAR AND TUNDRA REGIONS
The areas round the north and south poles are covered in ice. The temperature only rises above freezing point for a few months of the year. South of the north pole lie regions known as the tundra, where the lower parts of the soil are permanently frozen and only mosses and lichens can grow. As the climate is very dry, the tundra regions are sometimes described as cold deserts.

During the short summer period, the edges of the polar ice caps melt. Large pieces of ice break off and form icebergs.

MOUNTAIN REGIONS
The temperature in mountainous regions varies a lot – the higher up you go, the colder it becomes. Trees and plants often grow on the lower slopes of mountains, but above a certain height (known as the tree line), temperatures are too low for vegetation to survive. Still higher up is the snow line. Above this it is so cold that the ground is permanently covered by snow and ice.

Mt. Kilimanjaro in Tanzania lies almost on the equator, but it is so high that its peak is covered in snow all year round.

TAIGA
Taiga is a Russian word which means "cold forest." It is used to describe the huge areas of evergreen forest that stretch across northern parts of Canada, Scandinavia, and Russia. Evergreen trees, such as spruces, pines and firs, are the only type of vegetation that can survive in the long, snowy winters and short summers of this type of climate.

The trees in the taiga regions are an important source of wealth. They are used for timber and for making paper.

TEMPERATE FOREST
Much of northern Europe and parts of North America have a temperate climate, which means that the temperature is never very hot or very cold. Because these regions have rainfall throughout the year, they were once covered by forests. Most of these have now been cut down. Deciduous trees, which shed their leaves in the winter, are common in temperate regions.

Much of the land in northern Europe has been cleared for farming, and small pockets of trees are all that is left of the forests.

THE OCEAN FLOOR
The ocean floor is not flat. Like the land, it has many geographical features, such as mountain ranges, flat plains and deep trenches. The longest range of mountains in the world is the underwater Indian Ocean–Pacific Ocean Cordillera. It stretches from East Africa, through the Indian Ocean, around southern Australia, and across the Pacific Ocean to the Gulf of California – a distance of 19,200 miles (30,900 km). The deepest point in the oceans, the Mariana trench in the Pacific Ocean near Japan, is about 36,201 ft (11,034 m) below sea level – deeper than the height of Mount Everest. The shallowest parts of the oceans are the areas of seabed around the edges of the continents, which are called the continental shelves.

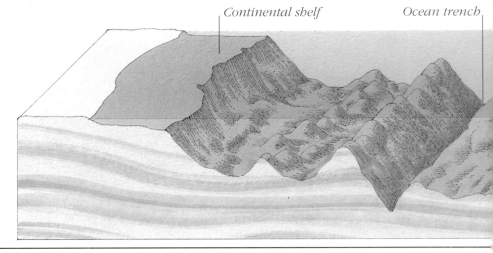

Continental shelf　　*Ocean trench*

MEDITERRANEAN

The name "Mediterranean" is given to the type of climate which is found around the Mediterranean Sea, and in other similar regions of the world, such as California in North America. These areas have hot, dry summers and cool, wet winters. The trees and plants that grow there are specially adapted to survive the lack of water in summer.

Olive trees are one of the few plants that thrive in this climate. They have been cultivated around the Mediterranean for many centuries.

DRY GRASSLAND

In the middle of some of the continents are huge plains of grassland, such as the North American Prairies, the Asian Steppe, and the Argentinian Pampas. These regions have extreme climates – very hot summers and very cold winters. Large parts of these areas have now been taken over for farming and are used for growing wheat or raising cattle.

South American farmers raise large numbers of beef cattle on the grassy plains of the Pampas.

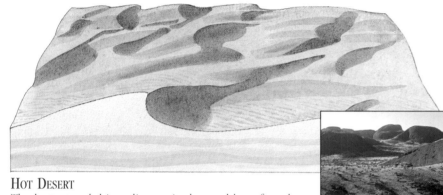

HOT DESERT

The hottest and driest climates in the world are found in the tropical deserts, such as the Sahara in Africa and the Australian Outback. The temperature there often reaches 100° F (38° C) in the shade. In some desert areas there may be no rain for several years. Deserts often contain sandy soil that can only support plants such as cacti, which are adapted to the dry conditions.

The dry, desert plains of the Australian Outback cover more than two-thirds of the continent. Few plants and animals can survive there.

TROPICAL GRASSLAND

Between the wet equatorial rain forests and the hot dry deserts lie regions of tropical grassland, such as the African Savanna. Here the climate is always hot, but the year divides between a dry and a wet season. Tall grasses and low trees and bushes grow in these areas. Tropical grasslands are grazed by large herds of plant-eating animals.

The African Savanna is the last place on earth where huge herds of grazing animals, such as zebras, gazelles, and wildebeest, still survive.

WHERE CLIMATES ARE FOUND

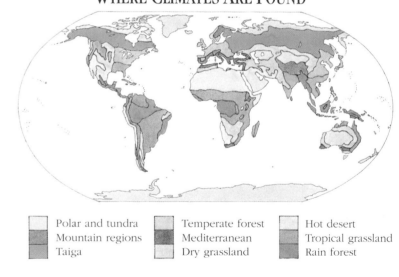

EQUATORIAL RAIN FOREST

In the regions around the equator, the climate is hot and wet all year round. The temperature remains constant at about 80–82° F (27–28° C). Vegetation thrives in this type of climate, and the equatorial regions used to be covered in dense rain forest. Much of this has now been cut down, although large areas still remain in the Amazon river basin in South America.

The Amazon rain forest covers an area 12 times the size of France. It is home to more species of birds and animals than anywhere else on earth.

☐ Polar and tundra	☐ Temperate forest	☐ Hot desert
☐ Mountain regions	☐ Mediterranean	☐ Tropical grassland
☐ Taiga	☐ Dry grassland	☐ Rain forest

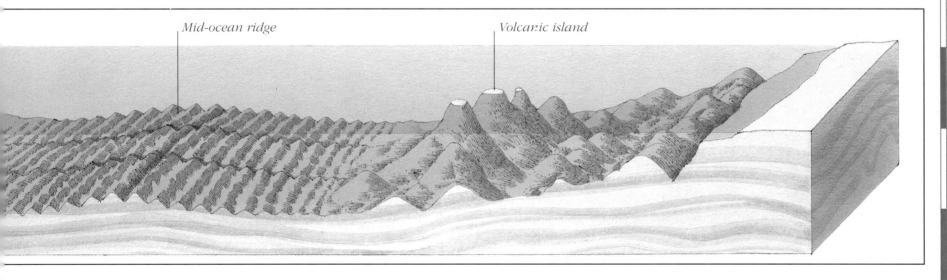

Mid-ocean ridge   Volcanic island

THE COUNTRIES OF THE WORLD

ALL OF THE CONTINENTS except Antarctica are divided into different countries, and these vary in size. By far the largest country in the world is Russia, which stretches across two continents – Europe and Asia. The second largest country is Canada and the third largest is China. At the other end of the scale, the smallest country is the Vatican City, which lies in the city of Rome in Italy. It has a total area of only 0.17 sq mile (0.44 sq km). Russia is more than 39 million times bigger than the Vatican City.

LATITUDE AND LONGITUDE

To help locate places in the world, geographers draw imaginary lines around the globe. Lines of latitude circle the globe from east to west. They are measured in degrees north or south of the equator. Lines of longitude circle the earth from north to south and are measured in degrees east or west of the line called the prime meridian.

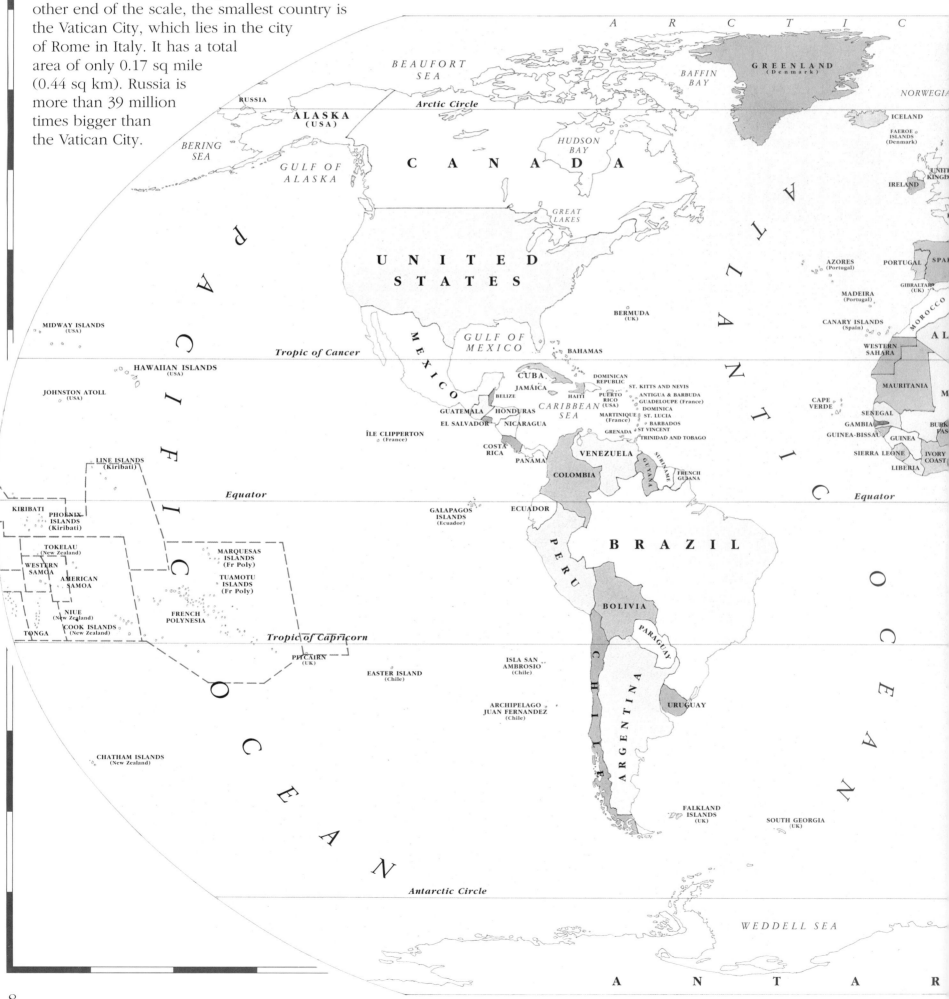

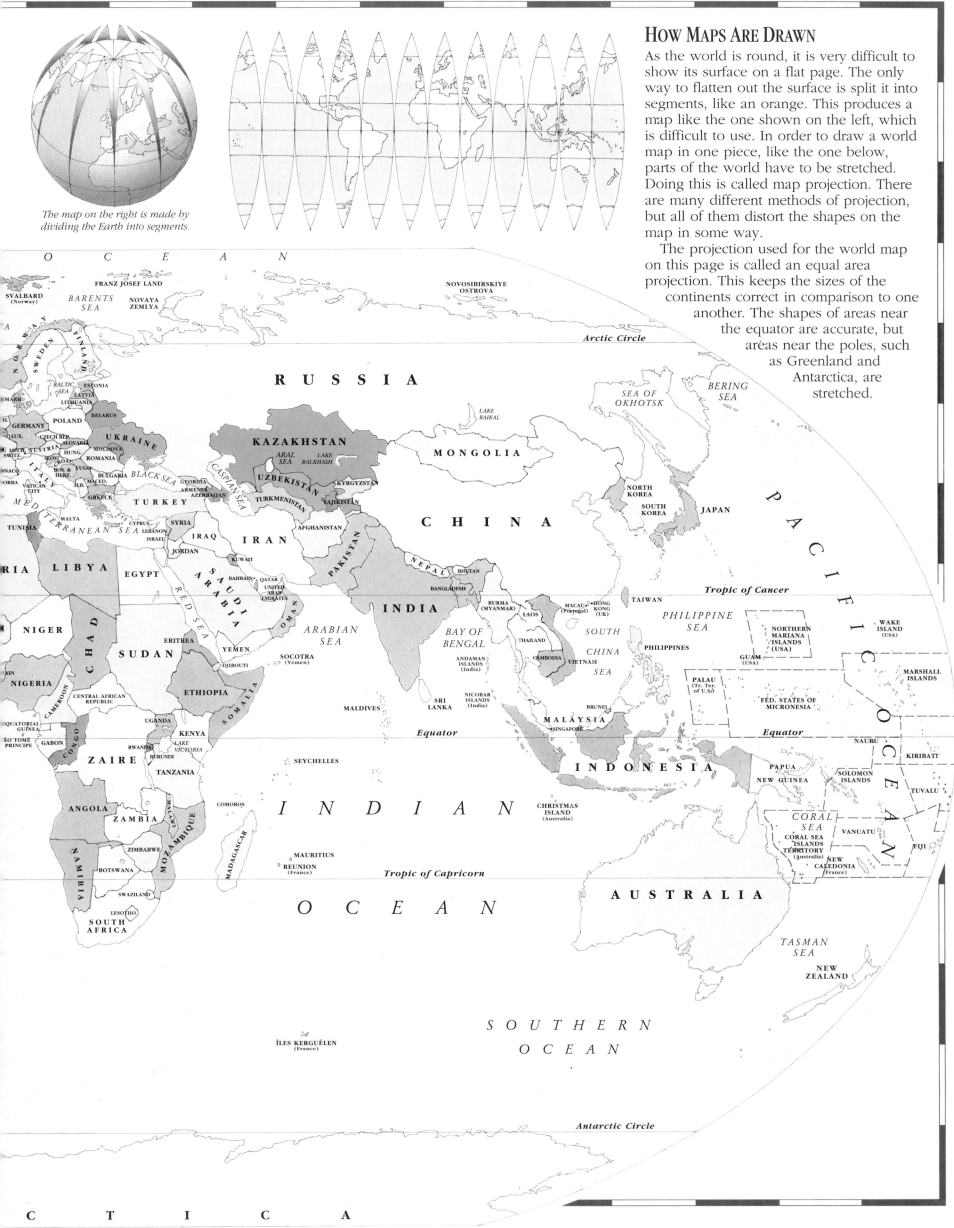

HOW MAPS ARE DRAWN

As the world is round, it is very difficult to show its surface on a flat page. The only way to flatten out the surface is split it into segments, like an orange. This produces a map like the one shown on the left, which is difficult to use. In order to draw a world map in one piece, like the one below, parts of the world have to be stretched. Doing this is called map projection. There are many different methods of projection, but all of them distort the shapes on the map in some way.

The projection used for the world map on this page is called an equal area projection. This keeps the sizes of the continents correct in comparison to one another. The shapes of areas near the equator are accurate, but areas near the poles, such as Greenland and Antarctica, are stretched.

The map on the right is made by dividing the Earth into segments.

THE BIGGEST, HIGHEST, AND LONGEST ON EARTH

WHAT IS THE LONGEST river on earth? How high is Mount Everest? Which is the world's biggest island? You can find the answers to all these questions below. Each of the sections is about one type of geographical feature – mountains, for example. The section contains the highest mountain on earth – Mount Everest – along with a selection of other mountains from around the world.

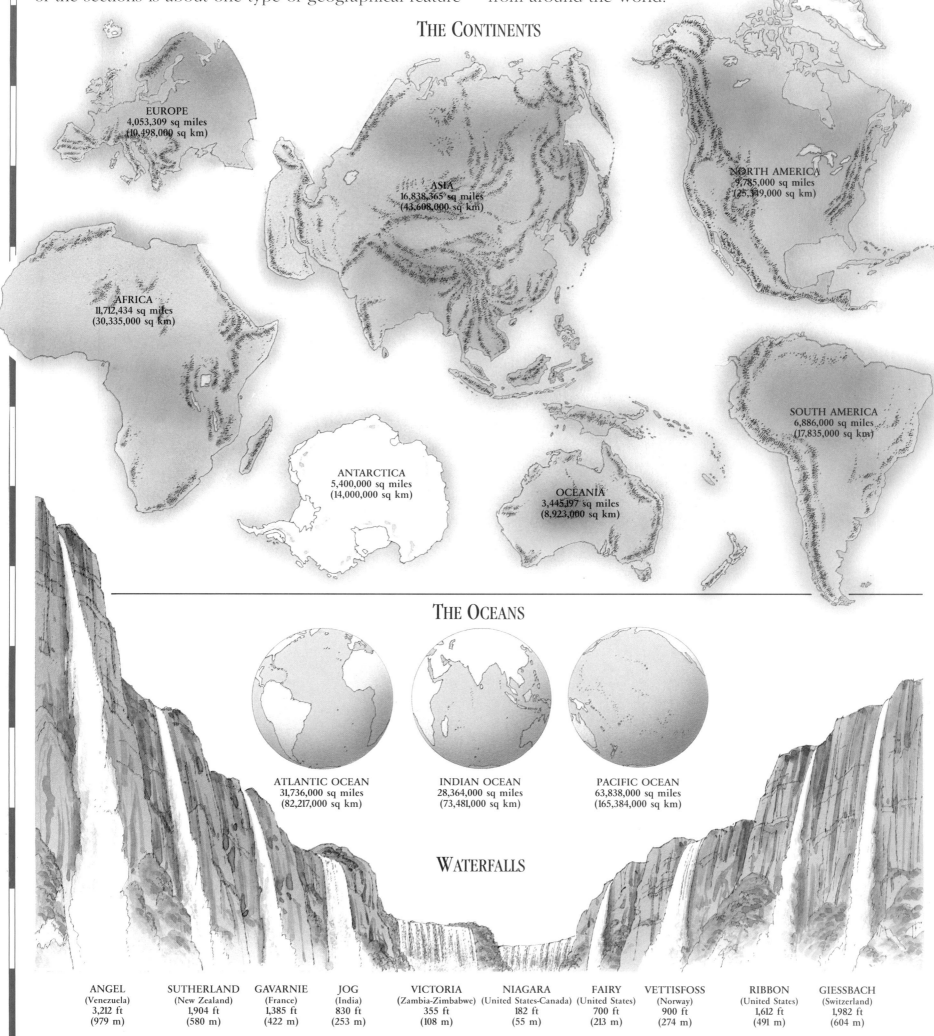

THE CONTINENTS

EUROPE
4,053,309 sq miles
(10,498,000 sq km)

ASIA
16,838,365 sq miles
(43,608,000 sq km)

NORTH AMERICA
9,785,000 sq miles
(25,349,000 sq km)

AFRICA
11,712,434 sq miles
(30,335,000 sq km)

SOUTH AMERICA
6,886,000 sq miles
(17,835,000 sq km)

ANTARCTICA
5,400,000 sq miles
(14,000,000 sq km)

OCEANIA
3,445,197 sq miles
(8,923,000 sq km)

THE OCEANS

ATLANTIC OCEAN
31,736,000 sq miles
(82,217,000 sq km)

INDIAN OCEAN
28,364,000 sq miles
(73,481,000 sq km)

PACIFIC OCEAN
63,838,000 sq miles
(165,384,000 sq km)

WATERFALLS

ANGEL (Venezuela)	SUTHERLAND (New Zealand)	GAVARNIE (France)	JOG (India)	VICTORIA (Zambia-Zimbabwe)	NIAGARA (United States-Canada)	FAIRY (United States)	VETTISFOSS (Norway)	RIBBON (United States)	GIESSBACH (Switzerland)
3,212 ft (979 m)	1,904 ft (580 m)	1,385 ft (422 m)	830 ft (253 m)	355 ft (108 m)	182 ft (55 m)	700 ft (213 m)	900 ft (274 m)	1,612 ft (491 m)	1,982 ft (604 m)

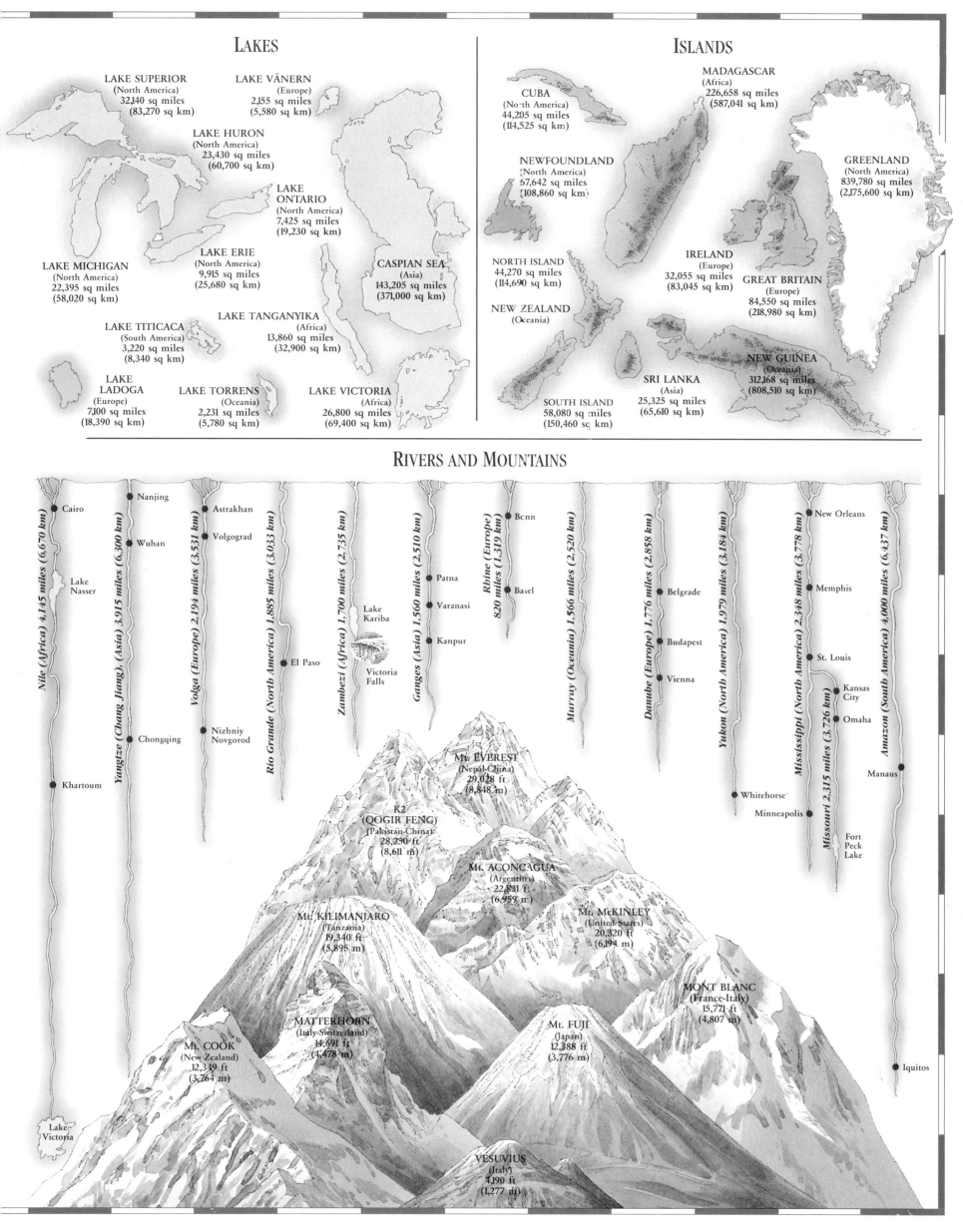

LAKES

LAKE SUPERIOR
(North America)
32,140 sq miles
(83,270 sq km)

LAKE VÄNERN
(Europe)
2,155 sq miles
(5,580 sq km)

LAKE HURON
(North America)
23,430 sq miles
(60,700 sq km)

LAKE ONTARIO
(North America)
7,425 sq miles
(19,230 sq km)

LAKE ERIE
(North America)
9,915 sq miles
(25,680 sq km)

LAKE MICHIGAN
(North America)
22,395 sq miles
(58,020 sq km)

CASPIAN SEA
(Asia)
143,205 sq miles
(371,000 sq km)

LAKE TITICACA
(South America)
3,220 sq miles
(8,340 sq km)

LAKE TANGANYIKA
(Africa)
13,860 sq miles
(32,900 sq km)

LAKE LADOGA
(Europe)
7,100 sq miles
(18,390 sq km)

LAKE TORRENS
(Oceania)
2,231 sq miles
(5,780 sq km)

LAKE VICTORIA
(Africa)
26,800 sq miles
(69,400 sq km)

ISLANDS

MADAGASCAR
(Africa)
226,658 sq miles
(587,041 sq km)

CUBA
(North America)
44,205 sq miles
(114,525 sq km)

NEWFOUNDLAND
(North America)
67,642 sq miles
(108,860 sq km)

GREENLAND
(North America)
839,780 sq miles
(2,175,600 sq km)

NORTH ISLAND
(North America)
44,270 sq miles
(114,690 sq km)

IRELAND
(Europe)
32,055 sq miles
(83,045 sq km)

GREAT BRITAIN
(Europe)
84,550 sq miles
(218,980 sq km)

NEW ZEALAND
(Oceania)

SRI LANKA
(Asia)
25,325 sq miles
(65,610 sq km)

NEW GUINEA
(Oceania)
312,168 sq miles
(808,510 sq km)

SOUTH ISLAND
58,080 sq miles
(150,460 sq km)

RIVERS AND MOUNTAINS

Nile (Africa) 4,145 miles (6,670 km) — Cairo, Lake Nasser, Khartoum

Yangtze (Chang Jiang) (Asia) 3,915 miles (6,300 km) — Nanjing, Wuhan, Chongqing

Volga (Europe) 2,194 miles (3,531 km) — Astrakhan, Volgograd, Nizhniy Novgorod

Rio Grande (North America) 1,885 miles (3,033 km) — El Paso

Zambezi (Africa) 1,700 miles (2,735 km) — Lake Kariba, Victoria Falls

Ganges (Asia) 1,560 miles (2,510 km) — Patna, Varanasi, Kanpur

Rhine (Europe) 820 miles (1,319 km) — Bonn, Basel

Murray (Oceania) 1,566 miles (2,520 km)

Danube (Europe) 1,776 miles (2,858 km) — Belgrade, Budapest, Vienna

Yukon (North America) 1,979 miles (3,184 km) — Whitehorse

Mississippi (North America) 2,348 miles (3,778 km) — New Orleans, Memphis, St. Louis, Minneapolis

Missouri 2,315 miles (3,726 km) — Kansas City, Omaha, Fort Peck Lake

Amazon (South America) 4,000 miles (6,437 km) — Manaus, Iquitos

Mt. EVEREST
(Nepal-China)
29,028 ft
(8,848 m)

K2 (QOGIR FENG)
(Pakistan-China)
28,250 ft
(8,611 m)

Mt. ACONCAGUA
(Argentina)
22,831 ft
(6,959 m)

Mt. McKINLEY
(United States)
20,320 ft
(6,194 m)

Mt. KILIMANJARO
(Tanzania)
19,340 ft
(5,895 m)

MONT BLANC
(France-Italy)
15,771 ft
(4,807 m)

MATTERHORN
(Italy-Switzerland)
14,691 ft
(4,478 m)

Mt. FUJI
(Japan)
12,388 ft
(3,776 m)

Mt. COOK
(New Zealand)
12,349 ft
(3,764 m)

Lake Victoria

VESUVIUS
(Italy)
4,190 ft
(1,277 m)

WHERE PEOPLE LIVE

THE TOTAL POPULATION of the world is more than five billion people. No one knows the exact figure, as it is constantly rising. The population of the world is growing faster now than ever before. It has doubled since 1950, and many experts believe that it will double again within the next 40 years.

The population of the world is not spread evenly around the globe. Many of the most densely populated countries are in Europe and Asia. In the Netherlands, for example, an average of 936 people live in each square mile of land. In contrast, Australia has an average of only five people per square mile.

POPULATION BY CONTINENT

The diagrams below show how many people live in each of the continents. Antarctica is the only continent which has no permanent population: the only people who live there are scientists and engineers.

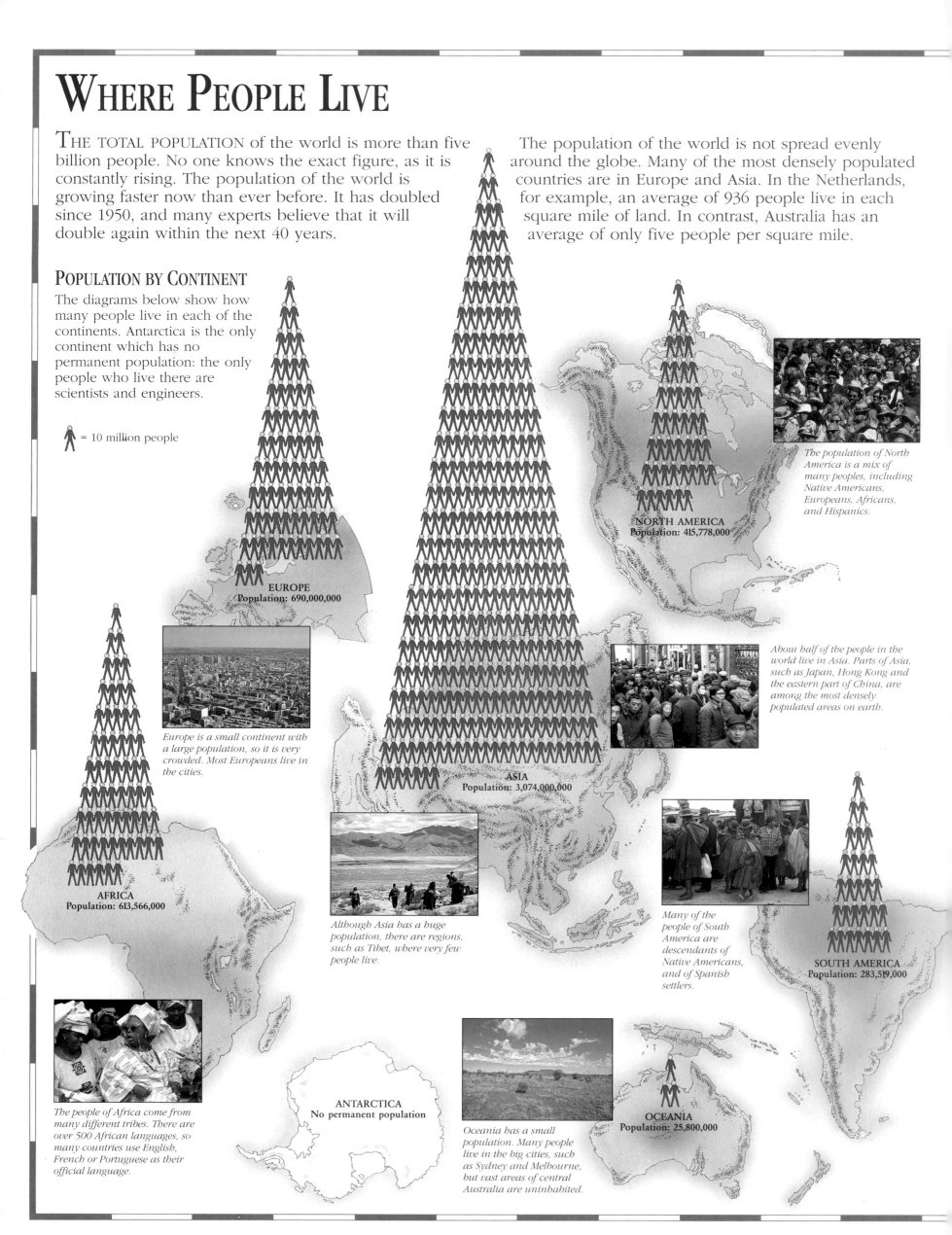

= 10 million people

EUROPE
Population: 690,000,000

Europe is a small continent with a large population, so it is very crowded. Most Europeans live in the cities.

AFRICA
Population: 613,566,000

The people of Africa come from many different tribes. There are over 500 African languages, so many countries use English, French or Portuguese as their official language.

ASIA
Population: 3,074,000,000

Although Asia has a huge population, there are regions, such as Tibet, where very few people live.

NORTH AMERICA
Population: 415,778,000

The population of North America is a mix of many peoples, including Native Americans, Europeans, Africans, and Hispanics.

About half of the people in the world live in Asia. Parts of Asia, such as Japan, Hong Kong and the eastern part of China, are among the most densely populated areas on earth.

Many of the people of South America are descendants of Native Americans, and of Spanish settlers.

SOUTH AMERICA
Population: 283,519,000

ANTARCTICA
No permanent population

OCEANIA
Population: 25,800,000

Oceania has a small population. Many people live in the big cities, such as Sydney and Melbourne, but vast areas of central Australia are uninhabited.

HOW TO USE THIS ATLAS

THE MAPS IN THIS ATLAS are split into a number of sections. There is one section for each of the continents: Antarctica, North America, South America, Europe, Asia, Africa, and Oceania. At the start of each section is a map of the whole continent, like the one of North America shown at the bottom of this page. Following this is a series of regional maps, like the one of France below, which show all the countries in that continent. This page shows how to use these maps and explains what the symbols on the maps mean.

NATIONAL FLAGS
The flags of all the countries on the map are shown like this.

BORDERING COUNTRIES
Countries which lie around the edges of the area shown on the map are colored yellow.

USING THE GRID
The grid around the outside of the page helps you to find places on the map. For example, to find the city of Paris, look its name up in the index on pages 77–80. Next to the word Paris are the reference numbers 39 E13. The first number shows that Paris is on page 39 of the atlas. The second number means that it is in square E13 of the grid. Turn to page 39. Trace across from the letter E on the grid and then down from the number 13. Paris is situated in the area where the two meet.

WHERE ON EARTH?
The red area on the globe shows where the countries on the map are situated.

FACTS AND FIGURES
This box contains interesting facts and statistics about each of the countries on the map.

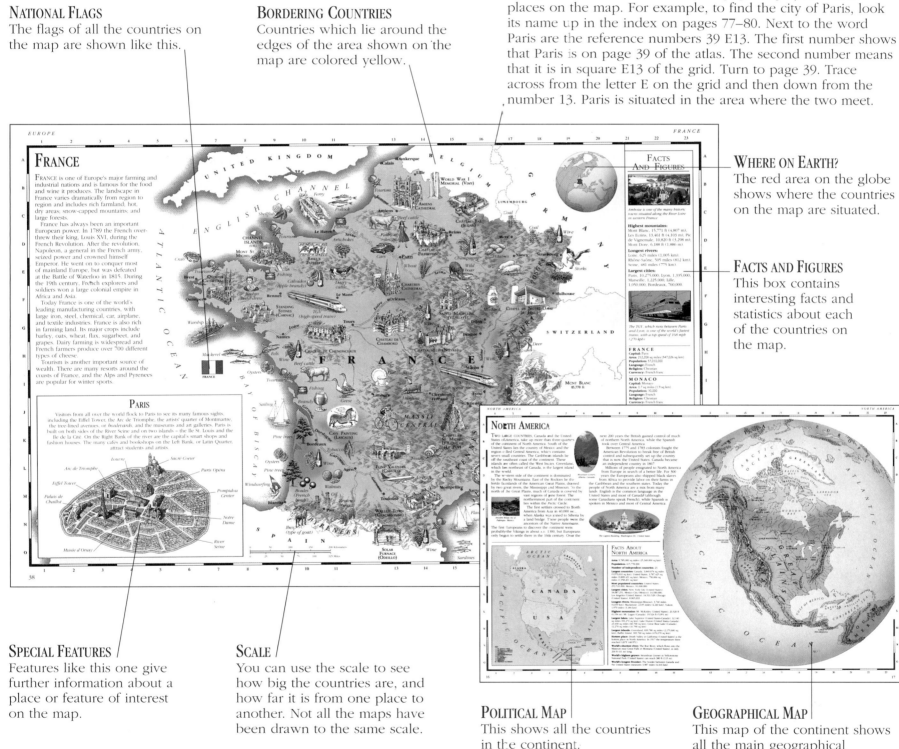

SPECIAL FEATURES
Features like this one give further information about a place or feature of interest on the map.

SCALE
You can use the scale to see how big the countries are, and how far it is from one place to another. Not all the maps have been drawn to the same scale.

POLITICAL MAP
This shows all the countries in the continent.

GEOGRAPHICAL MAP
This map of the continent shows all the main geographical features, such as rivers, mountains, lakes and deserts.

KEY TO THE MAPS

Capital City	City	Country name	Range of mountains	An individual mountain with its height	River	Lake	A specific building or place	A product, animal, plant or activity that is found all over the region
● LONDON	● Bristol	FRANCE	ALPS	△ MT. EVEREST 29,028 ft	Ganges	LAKE TITICACA	THE LEANING TOWER OF PISA	Wine

13

THE ARCTIC

THE ARCTIC CIRCLE contains the northernmost parts of North America, Europe and Asia, along with most of the island of Greenland. The temperature in the Arctic is so low that much of the Arctic Ocean is permanently frozen. Within the Arctic Circle, there are days in midwinter when the sun never rises, and days in midsummer when it never sets. Despite the harsh climate, a wide variety of animals and plants live in the Arctic. The main human inhabitants are the Inuit (Eskimos) and the Sami (Lapps).

The island of Greenland is anything but green – much of it is permanently covered by ice. The Inuit have lived in Greenland since about 2500 B.C. The first Europeans to settle there were the Vikings, in about A.D. 986. Today Greenland is a self-governing province of Denmark.

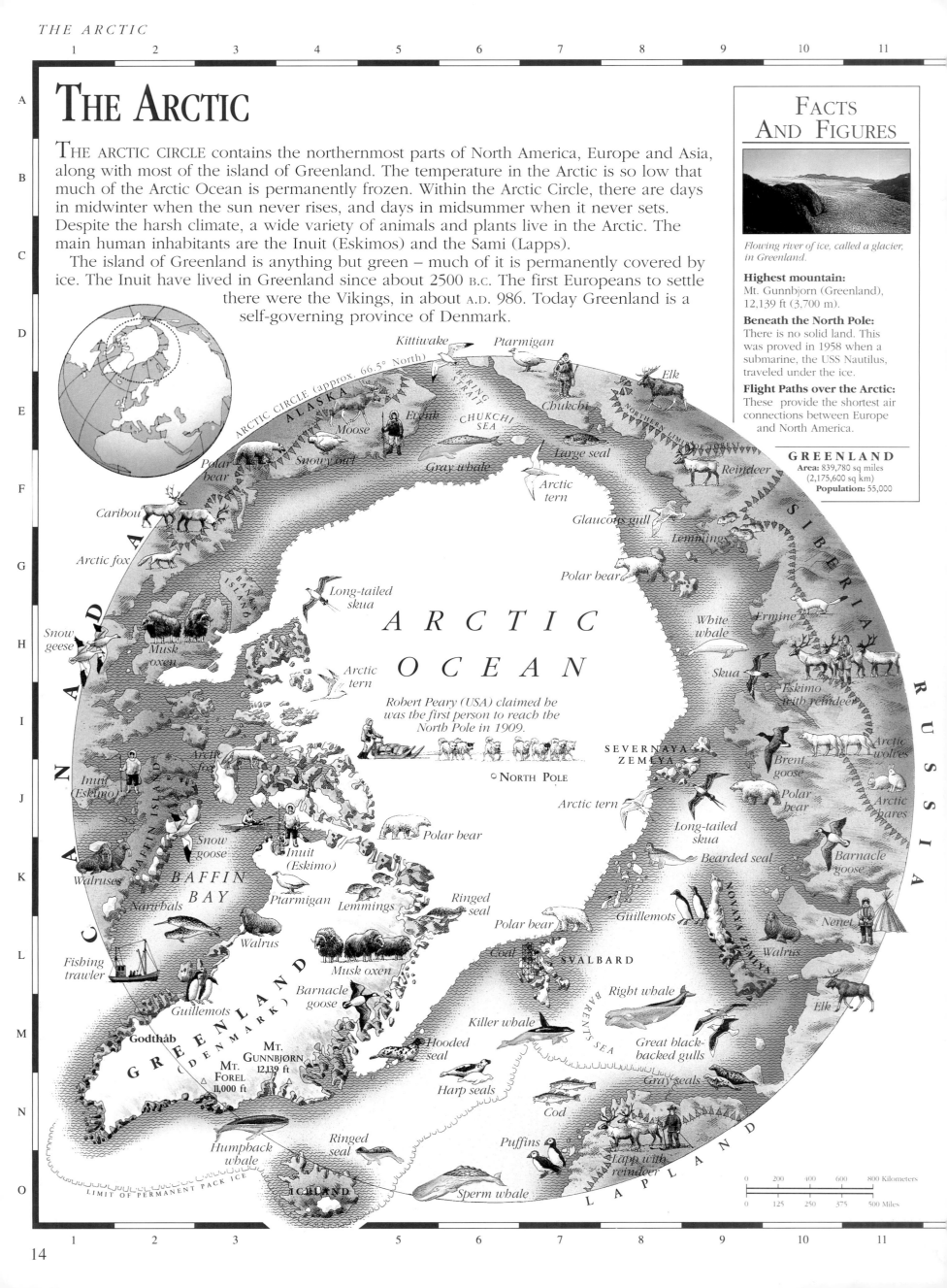

FACTS AND FIGURES

Flowing river of ice, called a glacier, in Greenland.

Highest mountain:
Mt. Gunnbjorn (Greenland), 12,139 ft (3,700 m).

Beneath the North Pole:
There is no solid land. This was proved in 1958 when a submarine, the USS Nautilus, traveled under the ice.

Flight Paths over the Arctic:
These provide the shortest air connections between Europe and North America.

GREENLAND
Area: 839,780 sq miles (2,175,600 sq km)
Population: 55,000

Robert Peary (USA) claimed he was the first person to reach the North Pole in 1909.

THE ANTARCTIC

THE ANTARCTIC has the coldest and harshest climate in the world. Nearly all the land is covered by ice, on average about 6,562 ft (2,000 m) thick. The size of the ice sheet varies between the seasons. In summer the ice at the edge of the sheet melts or breaks off to form icebergs. In winter the sea at the edge of the ice sheet freezes again and is called pack ice. There are very few plants. The animals that live in the Antarctic, such as seals and penguins, depend on the sea for their supply of food.

Although no country owns Antarctica, a number of countries claim territory, and many have bases there for scientific research. Even the small population of scientists dwindles during the bitter Antarctic winter, when blizzards last for days. The world's coldest temperature of -128.6°F (-89.2°C) was recorded at Vostok Station in July 1983.

FACTS AND FIGURES

The sea around the Antarctic is covered by drifting pack ice for most of the year.

Antarctica contains 90 percent of all the world's ice: If it melted, the level of the seas throughout the world would rise by 200 ft (60 m) and drown all the coastal towns and cities.

CONTINENT OF ANTARCTICA
Area: 5,400,000 sq miles (14,000,000 sq km)
Inhabitants: Scientists and engineers only
Climate: Cold, dry and windy

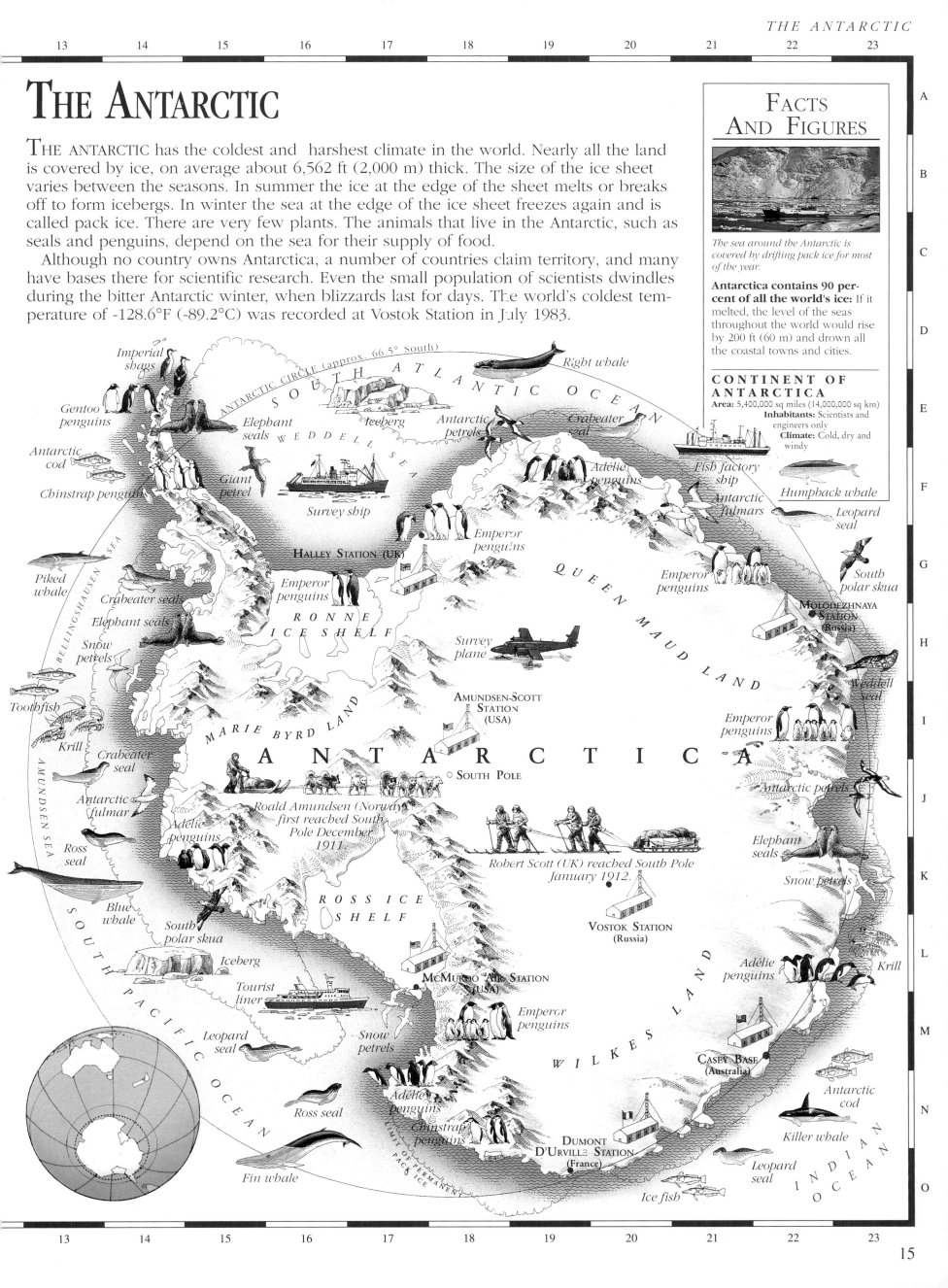

A

NORTH AMERICA

TWO LARGE COUNTRIES, Canada and the United States of America, take up more than three-quarters of the continent of North America. South of the United States lies the country of Mexico and the region called Central America, which contains seven small countries. The Caribbean islands lie off the southeast coast of the continent. These islands are often called the West Indies. Greenland, which lies northeast of Canada, is the largest island in the world.

The western side of the continent is dominated by the Rocky Mountains. East of the Rockies lie the fertile farmlands of the American Great Plains, drained by two great rivers, the Mississippi and Missouri. To the north of the Great Plains, much of Canada is covered by vast regions of pine forest. The northernmost part of the continent lies within the Arctic Circle.

The first settlers crossed to North America from Asia in 40,000 B.C., when Alaska was joined to Siberia by a land bridge. These people were the ancestors of the Native Americans.

The first Europeans to discover the continent were probably the Vikings in about A.D. 1000, but Europeans only began to settle there in the 16th century. Over the

Mountain scenery, Alberta, Canada.

Ancient Maya city of Palenque, Mexico.

next 200 years the British gained control of much of northern North America, while the Spanish took over Central America.

Between 1775 and 1783 colonists fought the American Revolution to break free of British control and subsequently set up the country that is now the United States. Canada became an independent country in 1867.

Millions of people emigrated to North America from Europe in search of a better life. For 300 years the Europeans also shipped black slaves from Africa to provide labor on their farms in the Caribbean and the southern states. Today the people of North America are a mix from many lands. English is the common language in the United States and most of Canada (although some Canadians speak French), while Spanish is spoken in Mexico and most of Central America.

The Capitol Building, Washington DC, United States.

KEY
1 ST. KITTS & NEVIS
2 ANTIGUA & BARBUDA
3 GUADELOUPE (France)
4 DOMINICA
5 MARTINIQUE (France)
6 ST LUCIA
7 ST VINCENT
8 BARBADOS
9 GRENADA
10 TRINIDAD & TOBAGO

FACTS ABOUT NORTH AMERICA

Area: 9,785,000 sq miles (25,349,000 sq km).

Population: 415,778,000.

Number of independent countries: 23.

Largest countries: Canada, 3,849,674 sq miles (9,970,610 sq km); United States, 3,787,425 sq miles (9,809,431 sq km); Mexico, 756,066 sq miles (1,958,201 sq km).

Most populated countries: United States, 253,510,000; Mexico, 91,000,000.

Largest cities: New York City (United States), 18,087,251; Mexico City (Mexico), 14.100,000; Los Angeles (United States), 14,531,529; Chicago (United States), 8,065,633.

Longest rivers: Mississippi-Missouri, 3,740 miles (6,019 km); Mackenzie, 2,635 miles (4,240 km); Yukon, 1,979 miles (3,184 km).

Highest mountains: Mt. McKinley (United States), 20,320 ft (6,194 m); Mt. Logan (Canada), 19,524 ft (5,951 m).

Largest lakes: Lake Superior (United States-Canada), 32,140 sq miles (83,270 sq km); Lake Huron (United States-Canada), 23,430 sq miles (60,700 sq km); Great Bear Lake (Canada), 12,270 sq miles (31,790 sq km).

Largest islands: Greenland, 839,780 sq miles (2,175,600 sq km); Baffin Island, 183,760 sq miles (476,070 sq km).

Hottest place: Death Valley in California (United States) is the hottest place in North America. In 1917 the temperature there reached 120°F (48.9°C).

World's shortest river: The Roe River, which flows into the Missouri near Great Falls in Montana (United States), is only 200 ft (61 m) long.

World's highest geyser: Steamboat Geyser in Yellowstone National Park (United States) can reach 380 ft (115 m).

World's longest frontier: The border between Canada and the United States measures 3,987 miles (6,416 km).

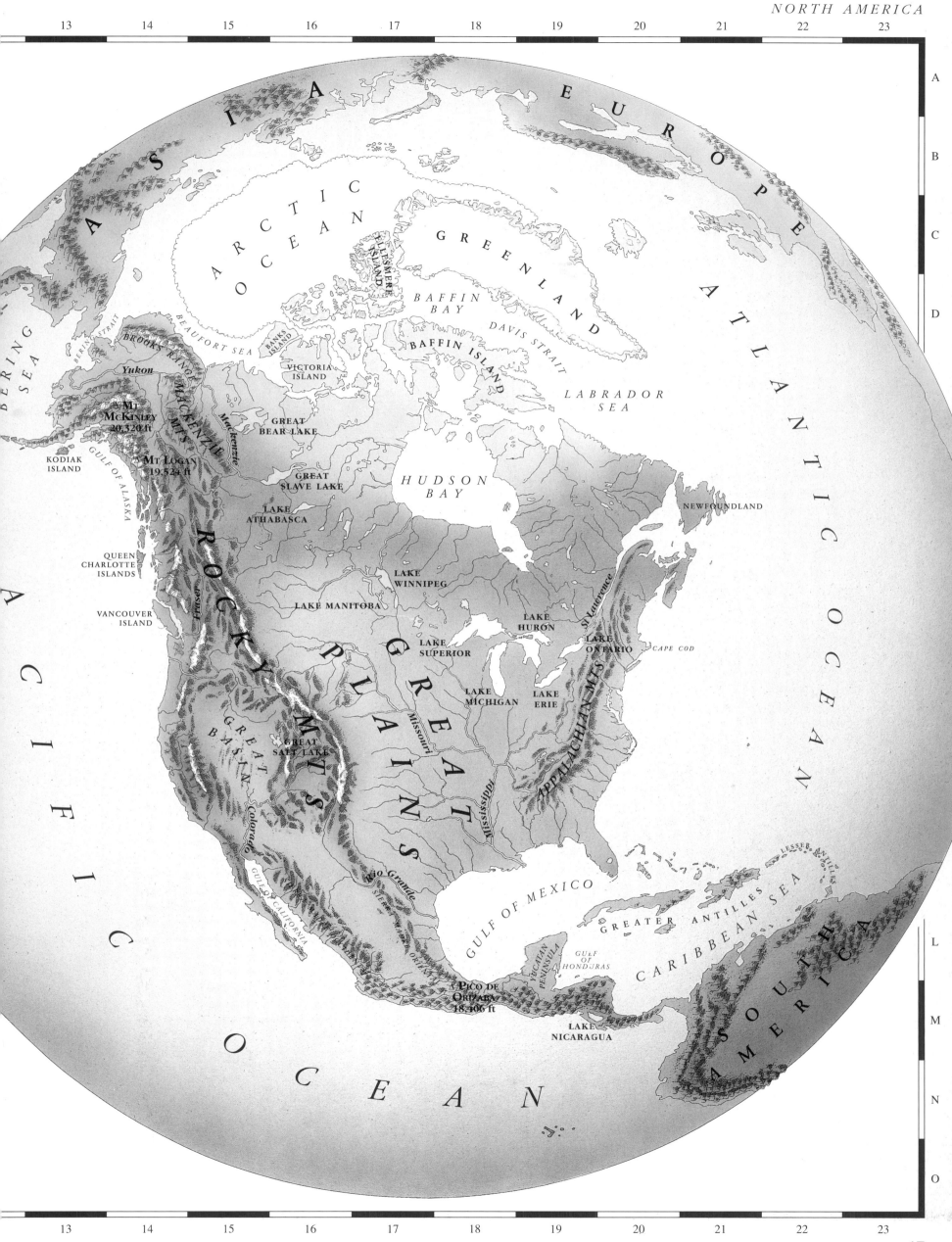

CANADA AND ALASKA

CANADA is the world's second largest country, yet its population is small – only about one-tenth the size of the smaller United States, its southern neighbor. More than half of all Canadians live in the area around the Great Lakes and the St. Lawrence River. In the center of Canada lie the Prairies, a flat plain used mainly for grazing cattle and growing wheat. Northern Canada is covered by vast areas of forest and tundra, while the west of the country is dominated by the Rocky Mountains.

The first inhabitants of Canada were the Indian and Inuit (Eskimo) peoples. French and British settlers started to move there in the 17th century. Although Canada became part of the British Empire, the French influence has always been strong and many Canadians still speak French today. Canada became an independent country in 1867.

Alaska, which lies to the northwest of Canada, is the largest state in the United States. Alaska is one of the world's major oil-producing regions.

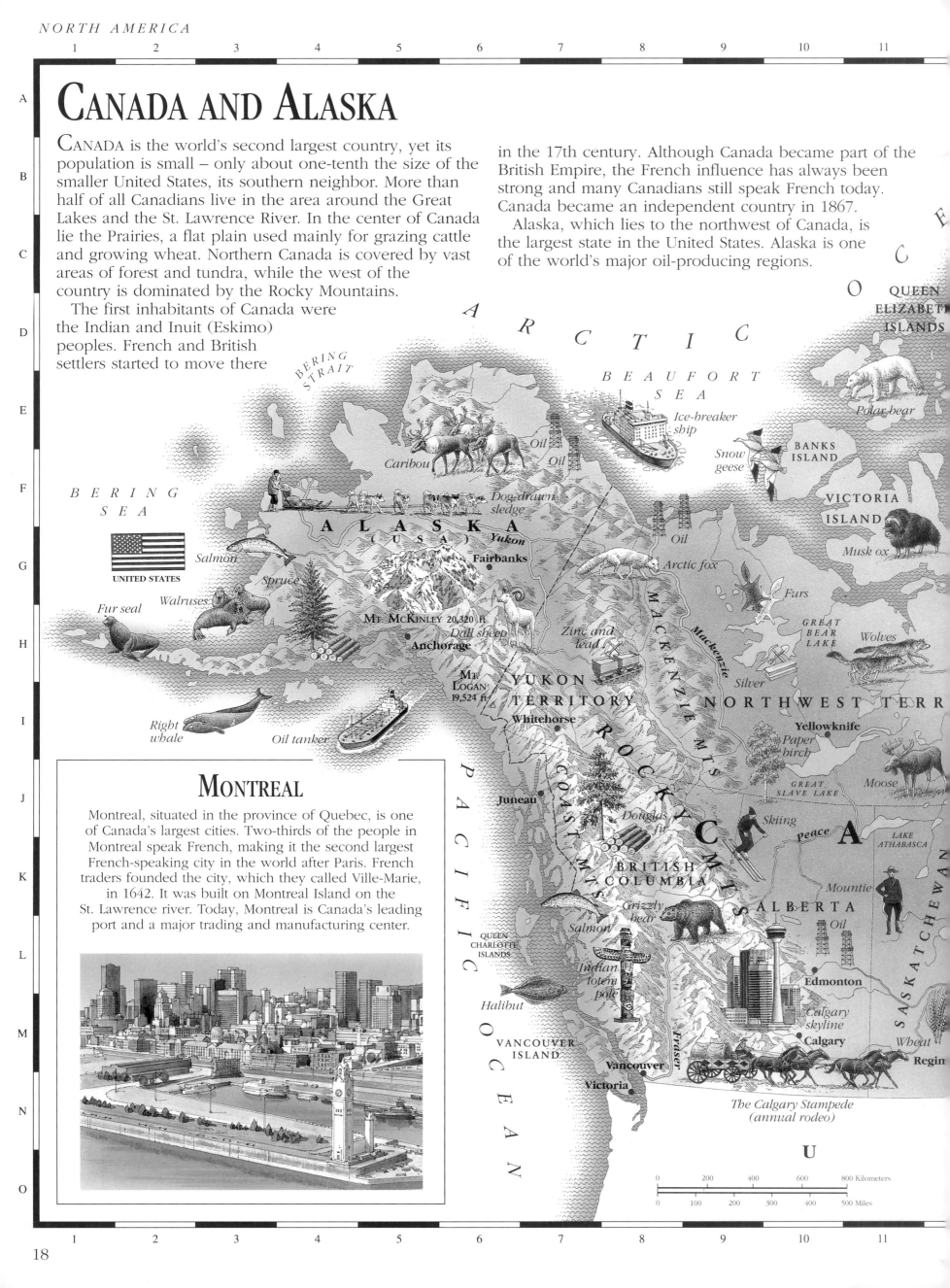

MONTREAL

Montreal, situated in the province of Quebec, is one of Canada's largest cities. Two-thirds of the people in Montreal speak French, making it the second largest French-speaking city in the world after Paris. French traders founded the city, which they called Ville-Marie, in 1642. It was built on Montreal Island on the St. Lawrence river. Today, Montreal is Canada's leading port and a major trading and manufacturing center.

UNITED STATES

BERING SEA
Fur seal
Salmon
Walruses
Right whale
Oil tanker
Spruce
Mt. McKinley 20,320 ft
Dall sheep
Anchorage
Mt. Logan 19,524 ft
Fairbanks
Yukon
ALASKA (USA)
Dog-drawn sledge
Caribou
BERING STRAIT

ARCTIC OCEAN
BEAUFORT SEA
Ice-breaker ship
Oil
Oil
Snow geese
Polar bear
BANKS ISLAND
QUEEN ELIZABETH ISLANDS
VICTORIA ISLAND
Musk ox
Arctic fox
Furs
GREAT BEAR LAKE
Wolves
Silver
Oil
MACKENZIE MTS
NORTHWEST TERR
Yellowknife
Paper birch
Moose
GREAT SLAVE LAKE
Mackenzie

YUKON TERRITORY
Whitehorse
Zinc and lead
ROCKY MTS
COAST MTS
Juneau
Douglas fir
Skiing
Peace
LAKE ATHABASCA
Mountie
BRITISH COLUMBIA
Grizzly bear
Salmon
Indian totem pole
QUEEN CHARLOTTE ISLANDS
Halibut
VANCOUVER ISLAND
Vancouver
Victoria
Fraser
ALBERTA
Oil
Edmonton
Calgary skyline
Calgary
SASKATCHEWAN
Wheat
Regin
The Calgary Stampede (annual rodeo)

PACIFIC OCEAN

| 0 | 200 | 400 | 600 | 800 Kilometers |
| 0 | 100 | 200 | 300 | 400 | 500 Miles |

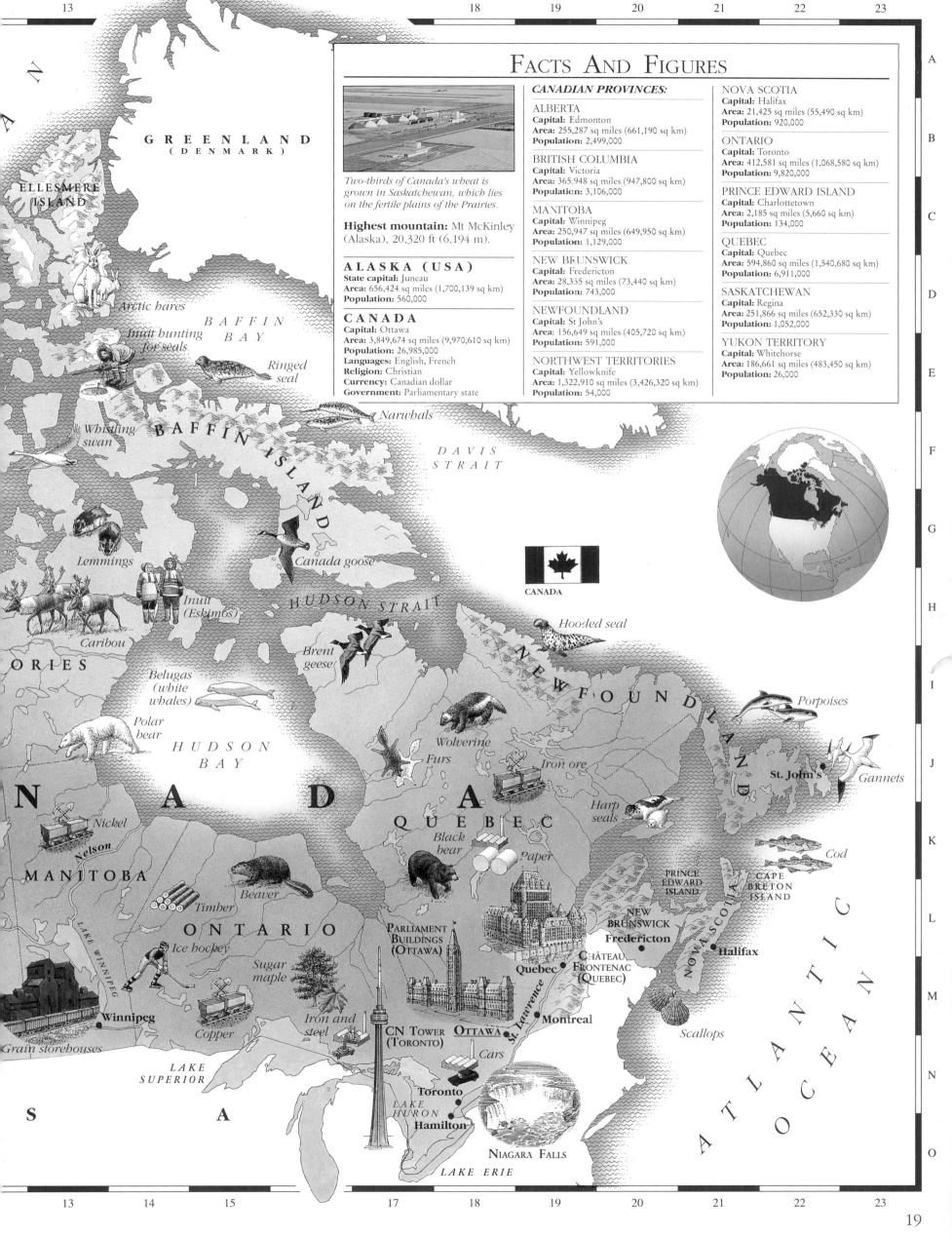

FACTS AND FIGURES

Two-thirds of Canada's wheat is grown in Saskatchewan, which lies on the fertile plains of the Prairies.

Highest mountain: Mt McKinley (Alaska), 20,320 ft (6,194 m).

ALASKA (USA)
State capital: Juneau
Area: 656,424 sq miles (1,700,139 sq km)
Population: 560,000

CANADA
Capital: Ottawa
Area: 3,849,674 sq miles (9,970,610 sq km)
Population: 26,985,000
Languages: English, French
Religion: Christian
Currency: Canadian dollar
Government: Parliamentary state

CANADIAN PROVINCES:

ALBERTA
Capital: Edmonton
Area: 255,287 sq miles (661,190 sq km)
Population: 2,499,000

BRITISH COLUMBIA
Capital: Victoria
Area: 365.948 sq miles (947,800 sq km)
Population: 3,106,000

MANITOBA
Capital: Winnipeg
Area: 250,947 sq miles (649,950 sq km)
Population: 1,129,000

NEW BRUNSWICK
Capital: Fredericton
Area: 28,335 sq miles (73,440 sq km)
Population: 743,000

NEWFOUNDLAND
Capital: St John's
Area: 156,649 sq miles (405,720 sq km)
Population: 591,000

NORTHWEST TERRITORIES
Capital: Yellowknife
Area: 1,322,910 sq miles (3,426,320 sq km)
Population: 54,000

NOVA SCOTIA
Capital: Halifax
Area: 21,425 sq miles (55,490 sq km)
Population: 920,000

ONTARIO
Capital: Toronto
Area: 412,581 sq miles (1,068,580 sq km)
Population: 9,820,000

PRINCE EDWARD ISLAND
Capital: Charlottetown
Area: 2,185 sq miles (5,660 sq km)
Population: 134,000

QUEBEC
Capital: Quebec
Area: 594,860 sq miles (1,540,680 sq km)
Population: 6,911,000

SASKATCHEWAN
Capital: Regina
Area: 251,866 sq miles (652,330 sq km)
Population: 1,052,000

YUKON TERRITORY
Capital: Whitehorse
Area: 186,661 sq miles (483,450 sq km)
Population: 26,000

CANADA

THE UNITED STATES

THE UNITED STATES OF AMERICA is one of the largest and richest countries in the world. It is made up of 50 states, each of which has its own government. The national government is based in the capital, Washington, D.C. The letters "D.C." stand for District of Columbia, the name of the area in which the city is situated.

The country is dominated by two mountain ranges – the Rockies in the west and the Appalachians in the east. In between lie the flat, fertile Great Plains, which are used for farming. The United States is rich in natural resources. It has large deposits of raw materials, such as iron, coal, and oil, which are needed to produce industrial goods. These resources have helped the country to become the world's greatest industrial manufacturer. The United States is also rich in farmland, and exports large amounts of agricultural produce, especially cereals, cotton, and tobacco. Most years, the United States exports more grain than all the other countries of the world combined.

The United States is often described as a "melting pot" because its population is a mix of many peoples. The country's first inhabitants were the American Indians. Later, settlers came from all over Europe, especially the UK, Italy, Ireland, and Poland. The United States' black population are the descendants of slaves who were brought to America from Africa. More recent arrivals include Hispanics (Spanish-speakers) from Mexico and South America, and Asians.

FACTS AND FIGURES

The area of New England is famous for its spectacular forests and old wooden houses.

THE UNITED STATES
Capital: Washington D.C.
Area: 3,787,425 sq miles (9,809,431 sq km)
Population: 253,510,000
Language: English
Religion: Christian
Currency: US dollar
Government: Republic

THE NORTHEASTERN STATES

THE NORTHEASTERN part of the United States is the most crowded region in the country. Large numbers of people live near the Atlantic coast in the big cities of Boston, New York, Philadelphia, Baltimore, and Washington. This coast was the first area of the United States to be settled by Europeans. In 1620 colonists from England, who are known as the "Pilgrim Fathers," established the first settlement at New Plymouth, Massachusetts, in the region that is still called New England.

Farther inland lie the Great Lakes, the largest group of freshwater lakes in the world, which form part of the border between the United States and Canada. The region around the Great Lakes has the greatest concentration of industry in the United States. The biggest cities are Chicago, Pittsburgh, and Detroit, which is known as the "Motor City" because it is the center of the American car industry. The main products of the area are iron and steel, machinery, cars, chemicals, coal, and textiles.

West and southwest of the Great Lakes are the states of Minnesota, Wisconsin, and Iowa, which lie on the flat land of the Great Plains. Much of the United States' wheat and corn is grown in this area, which is often called the "farm belt".

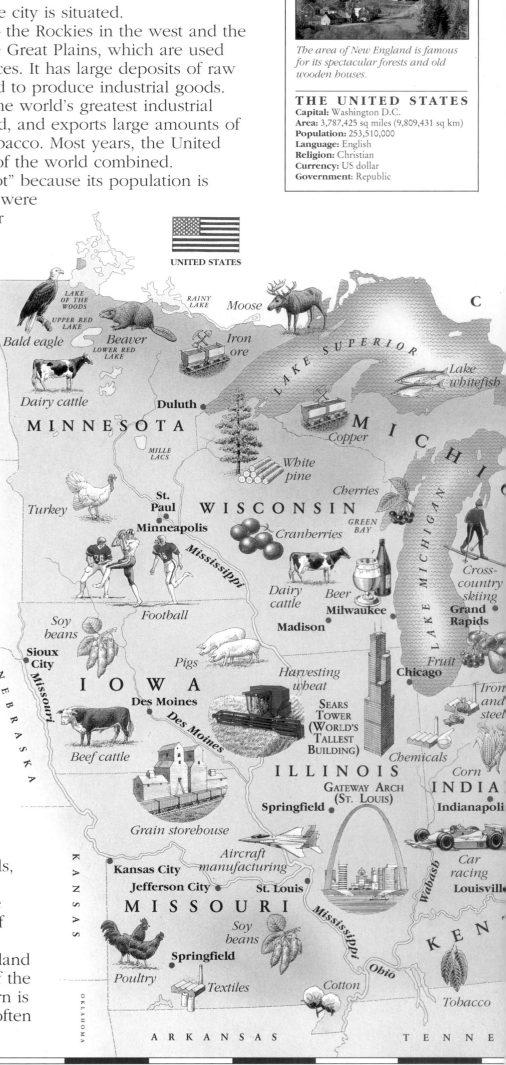

UNITED STATES

NEW YORK

The skyline of Manhattan Island in the center of New York is perhaps the best-known view of any city in the world. It was the first sight of America for the millions of people who emigrated there from Europe during the 19th and early 20th centuries. Today, New York is the largest city in the United States, the country's leading port, and a world financial center.

FACTS AND FIGURES

The skyline of Chicago is dominated by the Sears Tower – the world's tallest building.

THE NORTHEASTERN STATES:

CONNECTICUT
Capital: Hartford
Area: 5,544 sq miles (14,358 sq km)
Population: 3,336,000

DELAWARE
Capital: Dover
Area: 2,489 sq miles (6,447 sq km)
Population: 679,000

DISTRICT OF COLUMBIA
Area: 68 sq miles (177 sq km)
Population: 611,000

ILLINOIS
Capital: Springfield
Area: 57,918 sq miles (150,007 sq km)
Population: 11,575,000

INDIANA
Capital: Indianapolis
Area: 36,420 sq miles (94,328 sq km)
Population: 5,615,000

IOWA
Capital: Des Moines
Area: 56,276 sq miles (145,754 sq km)
Population: 2,801,000

KENTUCKY
Capital: Frankfort
Area: 40,411 sq miles (104,665 sq km)
Population: 3,727,000

MAINE
Capital: Augusta
Area: 35,387 sq miles (91,653 sq km)
Population: 1,252,000

MARYLAND
Capital: Annapolis
Area: 12,407 sq miles (32,135 sq km)
Population: 4,895,000

MASSACHUSETTS
Capital: Boston
Area: 10,555 sq miles (27,337 sq km)
Population: 6,107,000

MICHIGAN
Capital: Lansing
Area: 96,810 sq miles (250,738 sq km)
Population: 9,423,000

MINNESOTA
Capital: St Paul
Area: 86,943 sq miles (225,182 sq km)
Population: 4,459,000

MISSOURI
Capital: Jefferson City
Area: 69,709 sq miles (180,546 sq km)
Population: 5,200,000

NEW HAMPSHIRE
Capital: Concord
Area: 9,351 sq miles (24,219 sq km)
Population: 1,138,000

NEW JERSEY
Capital: Trenton
Area: 8,722 sq miles (22,590 sq km)
Population: 7,850,000

NEW YORK
Capital: Albany
Area: 54,475 sq miles (141,089 sq km)
Population: 18,260,000

OHIO
Capital: Columbus
Area: 44,828 sq miles (116,103 sq km)
Population: 10,980,000

PENNSYLVANIA
Capital: Harrisburg
Area: 46,058 sq miles (119,291 sq km)
Population: 12,042,000

RHODE ISLAND
Capital: Providence
Area: 1,545 sq miles (4,002 sq km)
Population: 1,019,000

VERMONT
Capital: Montpelier
Area: 9,615 sq miles (24,903 sq km)
Population: 583,000

VIRGINIA
Capital: Richmond
Area: 42,769 sq miles (110,771 sq km)
Population: 6,333,000

WEST VIRGINIA
Capital: Charleston
Area: 24,231 sq miles (62,759 sq km)
Population: 1,775,000

WISCONSIN
Capital: Madison
Area: 65,503 sq miles (169,653 sq km)
Population: 4,964,000

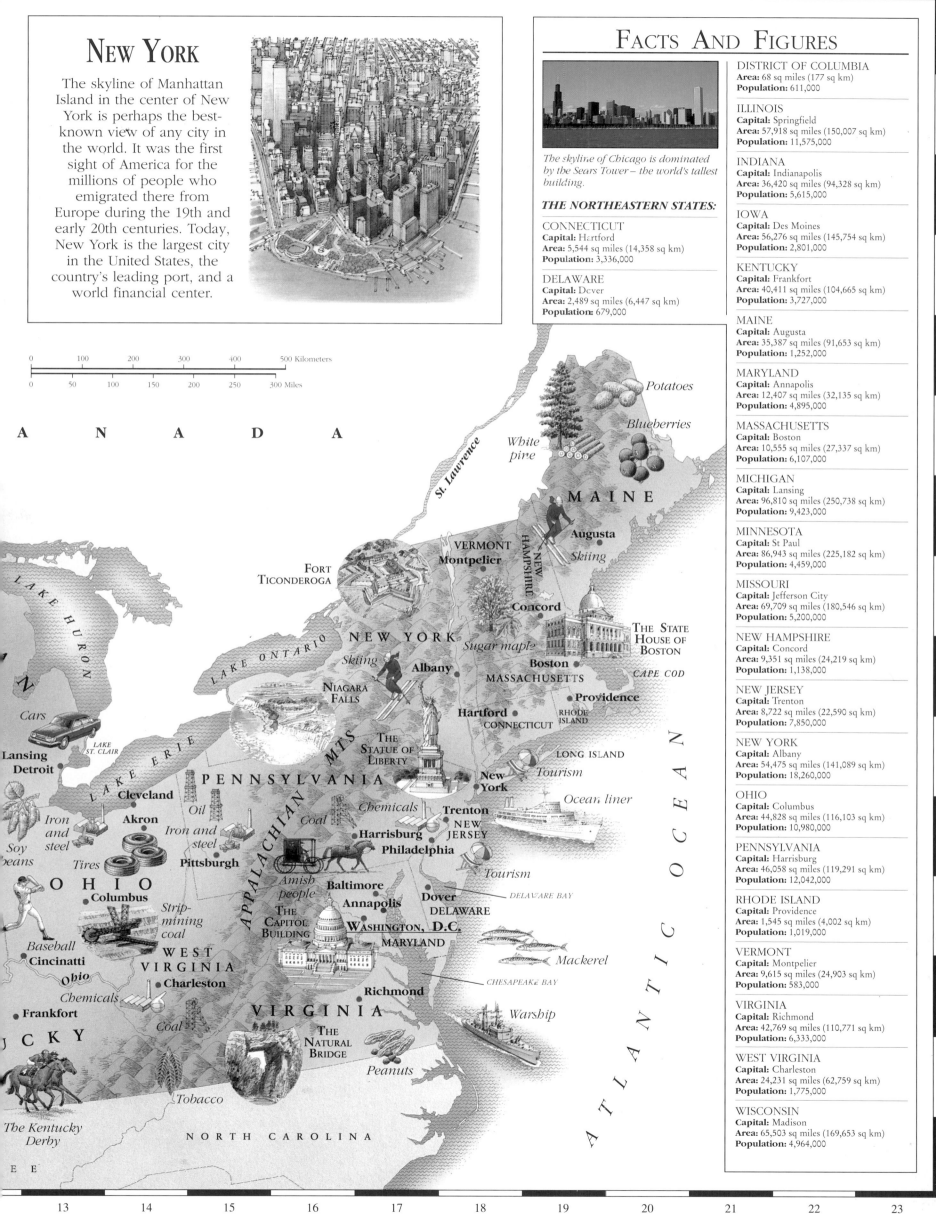

500 Kilometers
300 Miles

C A N A D A

St. Lawrence

White pine

Potatoes

Blueberries

M A I N E

VERMONT
Montpelier

NEW HAMPSHIRE

Augusta

Skiing

FORT TICONDEROGA

Concord

NEW YORK

Sugar maple

THE STATE HOUSE OF BOSTON

Skiing

Albany

Boston

MASSACHUSETTS

CAPE COD

NIAGARA FALLS

Providence

Hartford

RHODE ISLAND

CONNECTICUT

LAKE ONTARIO

LAKE HURON

Cars

LAKE ST. CLAIR

LAKE ERIE

THE STATUE OF LIBERTY

LONG ISLAND

Tourism

Lansing
Detroit

Cleveland

PENNSYLVANIA

New York

Ocean liner

Akron

Oil

Chemicals

Iron and steel

Iron and steel

Coal

Trenton

NEW JERSEY

Soy beans

Tires

Pittsburgh

Harrisburg

Philadelphia

APPALACHIAN MTS.

O H I O

Columbus

Amish people

Baltimore

Dover

DELAWARE

Tourism

Strip-mining coal

Annapolis

DELAWARE BAY

Baseball

THE CAPITOL BUILDING

Washington, D.C.

Cincinnati

Ohio

W E S T
V I R G I N I A

MARYLAND

Chemicals

Charleston

Richmond

Mackerel

Frankfort

Coal

V I R G I N I A

CHESAPEAKE BAY

Warship

KUCKY

THE NATURAL BRIDGE

Peanuts

A T L A N T I C   O C E A N

The Kentucky Derby

Tobacco

N O R T H   C A R O L I N A

THE SOUTHERN STATES

THE SOUTHERN STATES extend from the Atlantic coast in the east to the Mexican border in the west. Flowing southwards through the region is the Mississippi River, which reaches the Gulf of Mexico at New Orleans. Before the railways were built, the Mississippi was North America's most important trading route.

In the 18th and 19th centuries, the wealth of the South was based on farming. Cotton, tobacco, and other crops were grown on large farms called plantations. The workers on the plantations were black slaves, who were brought over from Africa. In the 1860s a civil war was fought in America between the southern states (the Confederacy) and the northern states (the Union). One of the main causes of the war was that the South refused to get rid of slavery. In 1865, the Union was victorious and the slaves were freed.

In the west of this region lies the huge state of Texas, which is famous for its cattle ranches and its oil. The long peninsula of Florida, in the south-east, is popular for vacations and attracts tourists from all over the world because of its good climate and beautiful beaches.

Natural gas · Wheat · Cotton · Armadillo · Dallas skyline · Diamonds · Amarillo · OKLAHOMA · Arkansas · Lubbock · Rodeo · Helicopters · Red · Football · El Paso · Fort Worth · Dallas · Shreveport · Oil · TEXAS · Electronics · Pecans · Oil · Cotton · Peanuts · Corn · Rio Grande · Waco · Brazos · Longhorn cattle · Cowboy · Petrochemicals · Rice · CHISOS MOUNTAINS · Austin · Colorado · Houston · THE ALAMO · San Antonio · Oil · MEXICO · SAN JOSÉ MISSION · Oil · Oil · Corpus Christi · Brown pelicans · Citrus fruit · Rio Grande · Shrimps · KANSAS · COLORADO · NEW MEXICO · GULF

Scale:
0 · 100 · 200 · 300 · 400 Kilometers
0 · 50 · 100 · 150 · 200 · 250 Miles

NEW ORLEANS – THE CITY OF MARDI GRAS

New Orleans is the oldest city in the South. It was founded by the French in 1718, passed to the Spanish in 1763, and finally became part of America in 1803. The city's mixed history is reflected in its population, which includes large numbers of *creoles* (descendants of the early French and Spanish settlers) and blacks. Early each year, New Orleans holds its famous carnival, called the Mardi Gras. During the carnival the city is filled with spectacular street parades and the sound of jazz bands.

13 14 15 16 17 18 19 20 21 22 23

ILLINOIS INDIANA WEST VIRGINIA VIRGINIA

SSOURI KENTUCKY

Country and western music

Poultry *Textiles* *Tobacco*

Soy beans **Greensboro** **Raleigh**

Nashville **Knoxville** *First powered flight by the Wright brothers*

Catfish T E N N E S S E E NORTH CAROLINA

Dairy cattle **Chattanooga** *Black bear* **Charlotte** *Sweet potatoes*

Cotton **Memphis** *Tennessee* APPALACHIAN MTS *Textiles*

ARKANSAS *Iron and steel* S O U T H

Little Rock *Coca Cola* **Columbia** C A R O L I N A *Tobacco*

Rice *Magnolia tree* **Atlanta** **Charleston** *Savannah*

Oil CONFEDERATE MEMORIAL (STONE MT) *Shrimps*

Mississippi steamer **Birmingham** GEORGIA *Soy beans*

M I S S I S S I P P I A L A B A M A **Columbus** *Cotton* **Savannah**

Jazz music **Jackson** *Alabama* *Cotton* *Flint* *Paper*

Raccoon *Peanuts* *Water-melons* *Yellowtail snapper*

Pearl *Oil* **Tallahassee** *Palmetto tree*

Mobile *Oil* *Chattahoochee* **Jacksonville** *Tourism*

L O U I S I A N A **Baton Rouge** *Apalachicola* F L O R I D A KENNEDY SPACE CENTER (LAUNCH SITE)

Oil **New Orleans** *Shrimps* *Cruiser* THE EPCOT CENTER (DISNEY WORLD) **Orlando**

Alligator MISSISSIPPI DELTA

Oysters *Lobster* **Tampa**

Oil rig THE EVERGLADES BAHAMAS

Anhinga (diving bird) *Tourism*

Fort Lauderdale

Miami

G U L F O F M E X I C O

FLORIDA KEYS

A T L A N T I C O C E A N

FACTS AND FIGURES

The city of Miami in Florida is a popular tourist resort. High-rise hotels line the beach.

Largest cities: Miami (Florida), 3,192,582; Houston (Texas), 3,711,043; Dallas-Fort Worth (Texas), 5,217,468; Atlanta (Georgia), 2,833,511; New Orleans (Louisiana), 1,238,816.

Longest river: Mississippi, 2,348 miles (3,778 km).

World's largest theme park: Disney World, in Florida, covers an area of 44 sq miles (113 sq km). Millions of people visit the park each year.

THE SOUTHERN STATES:

ALABAMA
Capital: Montgomery
Area: 52,423 sq miles (135,775 sq km)
Population: 4,099,000

ARKANSAS
Capital: Little Rock
Area: 53,182 sq miles (137,742 sq km)
Population: 2,383,000

FLORIDA
Capital: Tallahassee
Area: 65,758 sq miles (170,313 sq km)
Population: 13,360,000

GEORGIA
Capital: Atlanta
Area: 59,441 sq miles (153,953 sq km)
Population: 6,657,000

LOUISIANA
Capital: Baton Rouge
Area: 51,843 sq miles (134,275 sq km)
Population: 4,251,000

MISSISSIPPI
Capital: Jackson
Area: 48,434 sq miles (125,443 sq km)
Population: 2,604,000

NORTH CAROLINA
Capital: Raleigh
Area: 53,821 sq miles (139,397 sq km)
Population: 6,770,000

SOUTH CAROLINA
Capital: Columbia
Area: 32,007 sq miles (82,898 sq km)
Population: 3,559,000

TENNESSEE
Capital: Nashville
Area: 42,146 sq miles (109,158 sq km)
Population: 4,959,000

TEXAS
Capital: Austin
Area: 268,601 sq miles (695,676 sq km)
Population: 17,355,000

The state of Texas is famous for its huge cattle ranches, where cowboys still round up the animals on horseback.

13 14 15 16 17 18 19 20 21 22 23

THE WESTERN STATES

THE WESTERN part of the United States has the most rugged landscape in the country, with high mountains, deserts, and river canyons. The Rocky Mountains, which dominate the states of Idaho, Montana, Wyoming, and Colorado, mark where the West begins. The early settlers struggled across this difficult countryside in their wagon trains, but it was not until the railways were built during the mid-1800s that the American West was opened up.

California is situated on the Pacific coast and has the largest population of any of the American states. The first Europeans to settle there were the Spanish, as can be seen from many of the place names, such as Los Angeles, San Francisco, and San Diego. The central valley of California contains some of the richest farming land in the country. California lies on the San Andreas Fault, where two parts of the earth's crust are slowly moving in different directions. This movement causes frequent earthquakes.

HAWAIIAN ISLANDS (USA)

KAUAI
NIIHAU
OAHU
Honolulu
MOLOKAI
MAUI
LANAI
KAHOOLAWE
HAWAII

Surfing

Pineapples

KILAUEA VOLCANO

Gray whales

SAN FRANCISCO - THE CITY ON THE BAY

The city of San Francisco grew rapidly during the California Gold Rush of 1849, when miners flooded into California in search of their fortunes. In 1906 San Francisco was struck by an earthquake and large parts of the city were destroyed. Modern San Francisco is built on the hills around the bay.

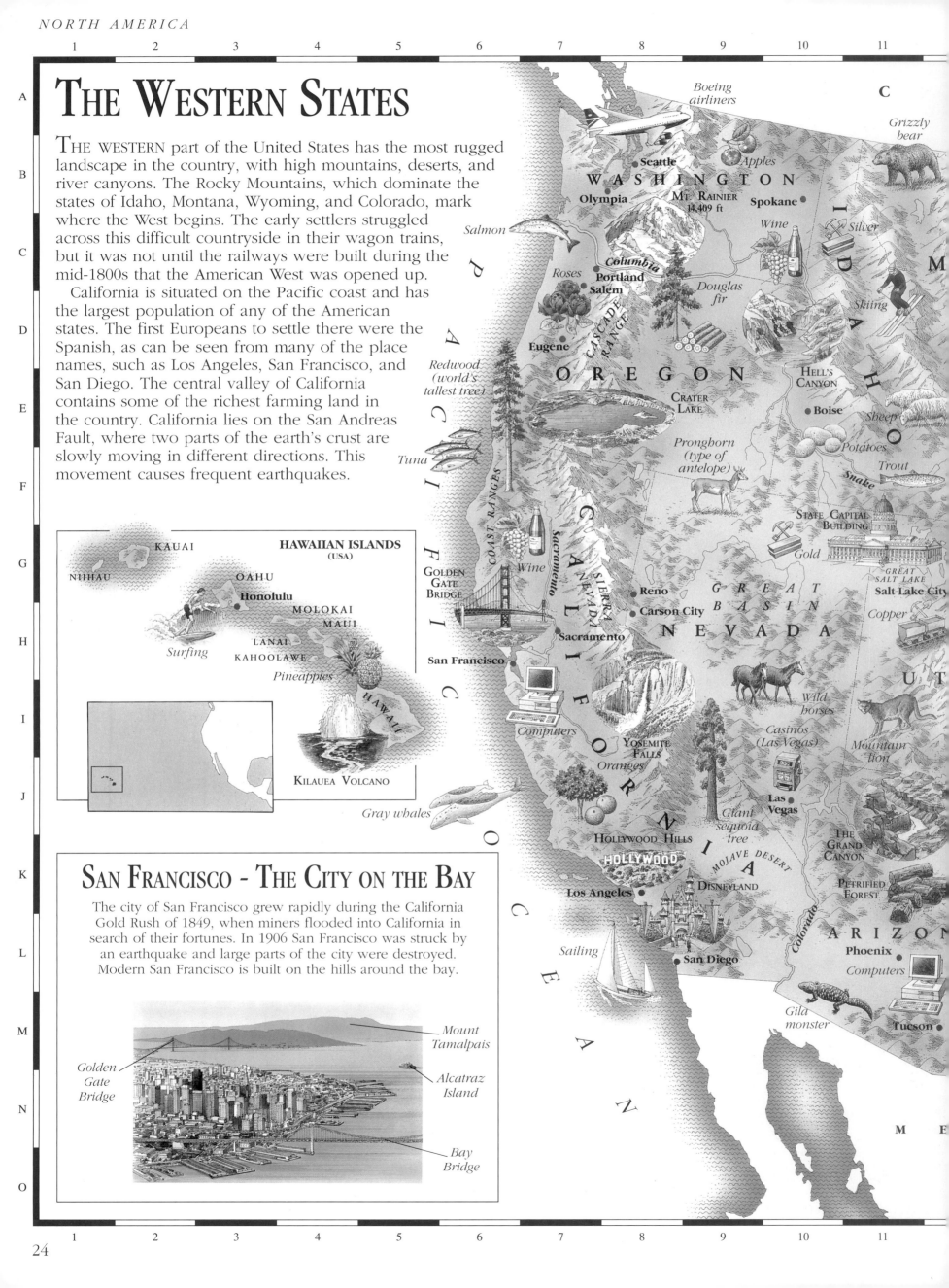

Golden Gate Bridge

Mount Tamalpais

Alcatraz Island

Bay Bridge

Boeing airliners

Grizzly bear

Seattle
Apples
WASHINGTON
Olympia
Mt. Rainier 14,409 ft
Spokane
IDAHO
Wine
Silver
Salmon
Skiing
Columbia
Roses
Portland
Salem
Douglas fir
Eugene
CASCADE RANGE
HELL'S CANYON
Boise
Sheep
OREGON
Crater Lake
Potatoes
Trout
Redwood (world's tallest tree)
Pronghorn (type of antelope)
Snake
Tuna
STATE CAPITAL BUILDING
Gold
Wine
Sacramento
GREAT SALT LAKE
Salt Lake City
GOLDEN GATE BRIDGE
Reno
Carson City
GREAT BASIN
Copper
Sacramento
NEVADA
San Francisco
Wild horses
UT
Computers
Casinos (Las Vegas)
Mountain lion
YOSEMITE FALLS
Oranges
Las Vegas
Giant sequoia tree
THE GRAND CANYON
Hollywood Hills
PETRIFIED FOREST
HOLLYWOOD
MOJAVE DESERT
Los Angeles
DISNEYLAND
ARIZON
Sailing
Phoenix
San Diego
Computers
Gila monster
Tucson

13 14 15 16 17 18 19 20 21 22 23

A N A D A

C A N A D A

Harvesting wheat

Wild ducks

Oil

Oil

N O R T H

Grand Forks

Missouri

Great Falls

O N T A N A

Helena

Oil

Yellowstone

D A K O T A

Bismarck

OLD FAITHFUL GEYSER (YELLOWSTONE NATIONAL PARK)

Oil

Wheat

Strip-mining for coal

DEVIL'S TOWER

Sunflowers

S O U T H

R O C K Y

D A K O T A

Wapiti (type of elk)

GANNETT PEAK 13,802 ft

Beef cattle

Pierre

Beef cattle

W Y O M I N G

MT. RUSHMORE

Prairie dog

Soy beans

Coyote (type of wild dog)

Cowboy

N E B R A S K A

Wheat

Omaha

Cheyenne

Skiing

CHIMNEY ROCK

Lincoln

Denver

Denver skyline

BUFFALO BILL'S RANCH HOUSE

Kansas City

C O L O R A D O

Topeka

RAINBOW BRIDGE

K A N S A S

Aircraft industry

Oil

Indian eagle dancer

SHIP ROCK

MONUMENT ROCKS

Wichita

Sorghum (cereal crop)

Oil

Rattlesnake

Oil

Beef cattle

Cotton

Oil

Tulsa

Santa Fe

Oklahoma City

Saguaros (giant cacti)

Albuquerque

N E W M E X I C O

O K L A H O M A

Bison

Corn

SOCORRO SPACE TELESCOPE

Rio Grande

T E X A S

CARLSBAD CAVERNS

SAN XAVIER DE BAC MISSION

X I C O

M I N N E S O T A

I O W A

Missouri

M I S S O U R I

A R K A N S A S

0 100 200 300 400 500 Kilometers
0 100 200 300 Miles

FACTS AND FIGURES

The city of Las Vegas in Nevada is famous for its nightclubs and gambling casinos.

THE WESTERN STATES:

ARIZONA
Capital: Phoenix
Area: 114,006 sq miles (295,276 sq km)
Population: 3,780,000

CALIFORNIA
Capital: Sacramento
Area: 163,707 sq miles (424,002 sq km)
Population: 30,680,000

COLORADO
Capital: Denver
Area: 104,100 sq miles (269,620 sq km)
Population: 3,356,000

HAWAII
Capital: Honolulu
Area: 10,932 sq miles (28,313 sq km)
Population: 1,133,000

IDAHO
Capital: Boise
Area: 83,574 sq miles (216,456 sq km)
Population: 1,065,000

KANSAS
Capital: Topeka
Area: 82,282 sq miles (213,110 sq km)
Population: 2,517,000

MONTANA
Capital: Helena
Area: 147,046 sq miles (380,850 sq km)
Population: 806,000

NEBRASKA
Capital: Lincoln
Area: 77,358 sq miles (200,358 sq km)
Population: 1,615,000

NEVADA
Capital: Carson City
Area: 110,567 sq miles (286,368 sq km)
Population: 1,257,000

NEW MEXICO
Capital: Santa Fe
Area: 121,598 sq miles (314,939 sq km)
Population: 1,550,000

NORTH DAKOTA
Capital: Bismarck
Area: 70,704 sq miles (183,123 sq km)
Population: 644,000

OKLAHOMA
Capital: Oklahoma City
Area: 69,903 sq miles (181,049 sq km)
Population: 3,169,000

OREGON
Capital: Salem
Area: 98,386 sq miles (254,819 sq km)
Population: 2,895,000

SOUTH DAKOTA
Capital: Pierre
Area: 77,121 sq miles (199,745 sq km)
Population: 673,000

UTAH
Capital: Salt Lake City
Area: 84,904 sq miles (219,902 sq km)
Population: 1,757,000

WASHINGTON
Capital: Olympia
Area: 71,303 sq miles (184,674 sq km)
Population: 4,984,000

WYOMING
Capital: Cheyenne
Area: 97,818 sq miles (253,349 sq km)
Population: 448,000

MIDDLE AMERICA

CENTRAL AMERICA is a narrow land bridge that joins the two continents of North and South America. At its narrowest point, in Panama, a canal 51 miles (82 km) long has been built to join the Atlantic and Pacific Oceans. There are seven small countries in Central America. To the north of it lies Mexico and to the east lie the hundreds of islands of the Caribbean Sea, which are often called the West Indies. This is a region of great variety and contrasts – large and small, rich and poor, old and new – with a fascinating mixture of different cultures and troubled histories. Modern Mexico City, one of the largest cities in the world,

lies on the site of an ancient city called Tenochtitlán, which was once the capital of the Aztec civilization.

On the Caribbean islands, tourist luxury and local poverty lie side by side. In the 16th century the islands were colonized by the Europeans, who shipped black slaves from Africa to work on the farms. Today the population is a mixture of many peoples. The main languages are English, Spanish, and dialects called *patois*, which are mixtures of African and French or English.

There are also great contrasts in the climate and vegetation of this area, from the Mexican desert in the north to the rain forests of the south, and the clear blue waters and coral islands in the east. Sometimes great tropical storms called hurricanes rage through the usually calm waters of the Caribbean. Winds of over 100 mph (160 kph) and enormous waves cause much damage.

TEOTIHUACÁN

Teotihuacán, located near modern Mexico City, was the capital city of an ancient Mexican civilization. Its name means "the city of the gods." At the height of its importance, around A.D. 600, it had 125,000 inhabitants and covered an area of more than 8 sq miles (20 sq km). The streets were laid out in a grid pattern and were lined with temples, palaces and about 20,000 houses. The huge Pyramid of the Sun, in the middle of the city, was one of the earliest religious centers in Mexico. In about A.D. 750 the city was destroyed by invaders and abandoned.

Map labels:

Tijuana · Mexicali · Cotton · Gila monster · Saguaro cactus · Copper · Ciudad Juárez · BAJA CALIFORNIA · GULF OF CALIFORNIA · Elephant seal · Hermosillo · Cattle · Chihuahua · Rattlesnake · Mexican with donkey · Armadillo · Rio Grande · Gray whales · Boojum tree · Sardines · Brown pelicans · Monarch butterfly · MEXICO · Gold · Torreón · Saltillo · Monterrey · Iron and steel · PACIFIC OCEAN · Shrimps · Huichol Indian · Folk dancers · Citrus fruit · Anchovies · Tuna · Flamingos · Lobster · GULF OF MEX · Grapes · Tampico · Oil · Shrimps · Aguascalientes · León · Guadalajara · NATIONAL CATHEDRAL (MEXICO CITY) · CHICHÉN ITZÁ (MAYA CITY) · Tourism · Tequila · Swordfish · Tourism · Fisherman · MEXICO CITY · Veracruz · Oil · Oil · Shrimps · Scarlet macaw · TIKAL (MAYA CITY) · Belize · Puebla · POPÓCATÉPETL VOLCANO 17,930 ft · Tzeltal Indian · BELIZE · Acapulco · OLMEC HEAD · Tourism · Aztec god · Quetzal · Coffee · GUATEMALA · GUATEMALA CITY · EL SALVADOR · SAN SALVADOR · Cotton · Shrimps

MEXICO

GUATEMALA · BELIZE · HONDURAS

EL SALVADOR · NICARAGUA · COSTA RICA · PANAMA

13 14 15 16 17 18 19 20 21 22 23

A
B
C
D
E
F
G
H
I
J
K
L
M
N
O

ATLANTIC OCEAN

U S A

FACTS AND FIGURES

Jamaica, which means "island of springs", is a popular tourist resort.

World's fastest population growth: The population of Central America has more than tripled since 1900.

ANTIGUA & BARBUDA
Capital: St John's

ARUBA
Capital: Oranjestad

BAHAMAS
Capital: Nassau

BARBADOS
Capital: Bridgetown

BELIZE
Capital: Belmopan

COSTA RICA
Capital: San José

CUBA
Capital: Havana

DOMINICA
Capital: Roseau

DOMINICAN REPUBLIC
Capital: Santo Domingo

EL SALVADOR
Capital: San Salvador

GRENADA
Capital: St George's

GUADELOUPE
Capital: Basse-Terre

GUATEMALA
Capital: Guatemala City

HAITI
Capital: Port-au-Prince

HONDURAS
Capital: Tegucigalpa

JAMAICA
Capital: Kingston

MARTINIQUE
Capital: Fort-de-France

MEXICO
Capital: Mexico City

NETHERLANDS ANTILLES
Capital: Willemstad

NICARAGUA
Capital: Managua

PANAMA
Capital: Panama City

PUERTO RICO
Capital: San Juan

ST. KITTS & NEVIS
Capital: Basseterre

ST. LUCIA
Capital: Castries

ST. VINCENT & THE GRENADINES
Capital: Kingstown

TRINIDAD & TOBAGO
Capital: Port of Spain

BAHAMAS   PUERTO RICO   BARBADOS   GRENADA   TRINIDAD & TOBAGO

CUBA   JAMAICA   HAITI   DOMINICAN REPUBLIC

Tourism

BAHAMAS

• **NASSAU**

Cruise liner

STRAITS OF FLORIDA

Scuba diver

Sugarcane

HAVANA •

Coral reefs

Coffee

Cocoa

TURKS & CAICOS ISLANDS (UK)

Coral reefs

Tourism

ANGUILLA (UK)

Frigate bird

VIRGIN ISLANDS (USA/UK)

ST. KITTS & NEVIS

ANTIGUA & BARBUDA

C U B A

Cigars

Pineapples

Pineapples

HAITI

PORT-AU-PRINCE •

DOMINICAN REPUBLIC

• **SANTO DOMINGO**

PUERTO RICO (US)

SAN JUAN

MONTSERRAT (UK)

Sailing

GUADELOUPE (Fr)

Coconuts

DOMINICA

MARTINIQUE (Fr)

Scuba diver

CAYMAN ISLANDS (UK)

JAMAICA

• **KINGSTON**

Reggae music *Rum*

Sharks

ST. LUCIA

BARBADOS

Green turtle

ST. VINCENT & THE GRENADINES

Nutmeg and mace

C A R I B B E A N   S E A

GRENADA

Steel bands

Grapefruit

HONDURAS

Cattle

TEGUCIGALPA •

Coffee

Bananas

NICARAGUA

MANAGUA •

Coffee

Coffee

ARUBA (Neth)

NETHERLANDS ANTILLES

TRINIDAD & TOBAGO

C O L O M B I A

V E N E Z U E L A

SAN JOSÉ •

COSTA RICA

PANAMA CANAL

PANAMÁ CITY

P A N A M A

Toucan

Spider monkey

0   200   400   600   800 Kilometers

0 100 200 300 400 500 Miles

27

Ancient Inca city at Machu Picchu, Peru.

SOUTH AMERICA

THE CONTINENT of South America is made up of great mountain ranges, thick forests, wide plains, and deserts. Running from north to south down the western side of South America are the snow-capped peaks of the Andes. These mountains are amongst the most recently formed on Earth and in places they are still slowly rising. Along the range of mountains are hundreds of volcanoes, some of which are still active. Many of the streams and rivers which join together to form the mighty Amazon River start in the Andes. The Amazon basin, which lies across the equator, is a hot, wet region which contains the largest tropical rain forest in the world.

The flat, fertile grasslands of the Pampas in the southeast of the continent are used for rearing cattle on huge farms called ranches, and for growing wheat. Farther south lies the colder, desert landscape of Patagonia. At the tip of the continent is Cape Horn, for centuries feared by sailors because fierce storms rage there for much of the year.

Saw mill on the Amazon River.

In 1498 Christopher Columbus became the first European to see the coast of South America. Europeans quickly colonized the continent, and until the beginning of the 19th century South America was ruled by Spain and Portugal. Argentina was the first country to gain its independence, in 1816. The people of South America are descended from American Indians, Europeans, and Africans. Spanish is the main language, except in Brazil, where Portuguese is spoken. Many Indians speak their own languages.

About half of South America's people make their living from farming. Most farmers grow just enough beans or corn for their families to live on, but there are large plantations where coffee, sugarcane, wheat, and other crops are grown. South America is also rich in natural resources, such as oil, gold, silver, copper, iron, tin, and lead.

Peruvians in national costume.

P

FACTS ABOUT SOUTH AMERICA

Area: 6,886,000 sq miles (17,835,000 sq km).

Population: 283,519,000.

Number of independent countries: 12.

Largest countries: Brazil, 3,286,488 sq miles (8,511,965 sq km); Argentina, 1,073,400 sq miles (2,780,092 sq km).

Most populated countries: Brazil, 156,750,000; Argentina, 32,860,000.

Largest cities: São Paulo (Brazil), 15,175,000; Buenos Aires (Argentina), 10,750,000; Rio de Janeiro (Brazil), 10,150,000.

Highest mountains: Mt. Aconcagua (Argentina), 22,831 ft (6,959 m), the world's highest extinct volcano; Ojos del Salado (Argentina-Chile), 22,615 ft (6,893 m), the world's highest active volcano; Mt. Bonete (Argentina), 22,546 ft (6,872 m).

Longest rivers: Amazon, 4,000 miles (6,437 km); Paraná, 2,796 miles (4,500 km); Madeira, 1,988 miles (3,199 km); São Francisco, 1,988 miles (3,199 km); Purús, 1,860 miles (2,993 km).

Main deserts: Atacama (Chile), about 50,965 sq miles (132,000 sq km); Patagonia (Argentina), about 300,000 sq miles (770,000 sq km).

Largest forest area: Amazon basin, about 2,700,000 sq miles (7,000,000 sq km).

Largest lake: Lake Titicaca (Peru-Bolivia), 3,220 sq miles (8,340 sq km). Titicaca is also the highest navigable lake in the world.

Largest island: Tierra del Fuego (Chile-Argentina), 18,140 sq miles (47,000 sq km).

World's wettest place: Tutunendo (Colombia) has an average annual rainfall of 463.4 in (11,770 mm).

World's driest place: Parts of the Atacama Desert (Chile) have an average annual rainfall of nil. In 1971 rain fell there for the first time in over 400 years.

World's highest waterfall: Angel Falls on the River Carrao (Venezuela) has a total drop of 3,212 ft (979 m).

World's largest lagoon: Lagoa dos Patos (Brazil) covers 4,110 sq miles (10,645 sq km).

NORTH AMERICA

ATLANTIC OCEAN

GULF OF MEXICO

GREATER ANTILLES

LESSER ANTILLES

CARIBBEAN SEA

CENTRAL
AMERICA

AFRICA

GALAPAGOS
ISLANDS

PACIFIC OCEAN

GULF OF
PANAMA

LAKE
MARACAIBO

Orinoco

GUIANA HIGHLANDS

MARAJÓ ISLAND

Negro

Amazon

AMAZON
BASIN

Tocantins

Parnaíba

Purús

Madeira

MT. HUASCARAN 22,133 ft

São Francisco

MATO
GROSSO

BRAZILIAN
HIGHLANDS

LAKE
TITICACA

LAKE
POOPÓ

ATACAMA DESERT

GRAN CHACO

Paraguay

Paraná

OJOS DEL SALADO
22,615 ft

MT. BONETE
22,546 ft

Paraná

Uruguay

LAGOA DOS
PATOS

TRINIDADE

MT. ACONCAGUA
22,831 ft

Paraná

RÍO DE LA PLATA

PAMPAS

PATAGONIA

BAHÍA BLANCA

GULF OF ST MATÍAS

TRISTAN
DA CUNHA

FALKLAND ISLANDS
(ISLAS MALVINAS)

TIERRA DEL
FUEGO

SOUTH
GEORGIA

CAPE
HORN

DRAKE PASSAGE

SOUTH SHETLAND
ISLANDS

SOUTH
SANDWICH
ISLANDS

ANTARCTICA

ANDES

A

B

C

D

L

M

N

O

NORTHERN SOUTH AMERICA

THE NORTHERN PART of South America is dominated by the vast, humid Amazon rain forest and by the high, snow-capped Andes Mountains in the west. The Amazon River is the second longest in the world, after the Nile, and runs for 4,000 miles (6,437 km) from its source in the Peruvian Andes to its mouth in northern Brazil. Every hour the Amazon delivers an average of 170 billion gallons (773 billion liters) of water into the Atlantic.

The Andes region of Peru was the center of the great Inca empire, which flourished in the 15th and 16th centuries. It was destroyed in 1532-33 by the Spanish conquistadors, led by Francisco Pizarro. The Incas were brilliant engineers, building roads and canals through difficult mountain landscapes. They were also skilled scientists, craftsmen, and farmers.

Brazil is by far the largest country in South America, both in size and population. In the overcrowded cities of southeast Brazil, such as São Paulo and Rio de Janeiro, large numbers of poor people live in slums known as "favelas."

In recent years, political and social problems have caused much upheaval in this region. Some of the nations are ruled by dictators. Colombia is one of the most dangerous countries in the world because of its ruthless drug trade. Tourism, however, remains an important source of income in South America.

THE AMAZON RAIN FOREST

The Amazon rain forest covers an area larger than Western Europe and supports more than one-fifth of the world's plant and animal species. It is also the home of tribes of Indians who have lived there for thousands of years. But each year about 77,200 sq miles (200,000 sq km) of forest is cut down for farming and mining. As a result of the destruction of the forest, many of the plants and animals are disappearing.

GALAPAGOS ISLANDS
(ECUADOR)

13 14 15 16 17 18 19 20 21 22 23

VENEZUELA

GUYANA

SURINAME

FRENCH GUIANA

200 400 600 800 1000 Kilometers

150 300 450 600 Miles

A T L A N T I C   O C E A N

GEORGETOWN

Sugarcane

PARAMARIBO

ARIANE ROCKET LAUNCH SITE

SURINAME

CAYENNE

FRENCH GUIANA

Green turtle

Wayana Indian

Water buffalo

Lobster

BRAZIL

MANAUS OPERA HOUSE

MARAJÓ ISLAND

Belém

Jangada fishing raft

Manaus

Amazon

Gold and blue macaw

Mango tree

Coconut palms

Gold

Xingu

Fortaleza

Tourism

Anaconda

Bananas

Teresina

Brazil nuts

Natal

Caiman

Kayapo Indian

CHURCH OF OUR LADY OF CARMO

Recife

Suya Indian

Tapir

Tourism

Umbrella bird

B R A Z I L

Tocantins

São Francisco

Araguaia

Marmoset

Giant armadillo

BRAZILIA CATHEDRAL DOME

Sugarcane

Salvador

Cocoa pods

M A T O G R O S S O

Cuiabá

BRASÍLIA

Gold

Shrimps

A

Cattle

Tourism

Campo Grande

Coffee

Soccer

Hummingbird

Belo Horizonte

Jabiru stork

Carnival

Wheat

Campinas

Rio de Janeiro

CORCOVADO STATUE OF CHRIST

SUGAR LOAF MT 1,295 ft

São Paulo

Cars

Curitiba

Tourism

Gaucho (cattleherder)

Paraná

Hake

PORTO ALEGRE CATHEDRAL

Porto Alegre

Soy beans

FACTS AND FIGURES

Traditional reed boats are still used on Lake Titicaca, the highest navigable lake in the world.

Highest mountains:
Mt. Huascarán (Peru), 22,133 ft (6,768 m); Mt. Sajama (Bolivia), 21,463 ft (6,542 m).

Longest rivers:
Amazon, 4,000 miles (6,437 km); Madeira, 1,988 miles (3,199 km); São Francisco, 1,988 miles (3,199 km); Purús, 1,860 miles (2,993 km).

Largest lake: Lake Titicaca (Peru-Bolivia), 3,220 sq miles (8,340 sq km).

World's highest waterfall: Angel Falls (Venezuela), 3,212 ft (979 m).

Largest cities:
São Paulo (Brazil), 15,175,000; Rio de Janeiro (Brazil), 10,150,000; Lima (Peru), 4,608,010.

World's leading coffee grower:
Brazil grows around 3,936,826 tons (4,000,000 tonnes) of coffee each year.

Sugar Loaf Mountain stands at the entrance to Rio de Janeiro's harbor.

BOLIVIA
Capital and seat of government: La Paz
Seat of judiciary: Sucre
Area: 424,165 sq miles (1,098,581 sq km)
Population: 7,243,000

BRAZIL
Capital: Brasília
Area: 3,286,488 sq miles (8,511,965 sq km)
Population: 156,750,000

COLOMBIA
Capital: Santa Fe de Bogotá
Area: 440,831 sq miles (1,141,748 sq km)
Population: 33,170,000

ECUADOR
Capital: Quito
Area: 109,484 sq miles (283,561 sq km)
Population: 10,880,000

FRENCH GUIANA
Capital: Cayenne
Area: 35,135 sq miles (91,000 sq km)
Population: 104,000

GUYANA
Capital: Georgetown
Area: 83,000 sq miles (214,969 sq km)
Population: 748,000

PERU
Capital: Lima
Area: 496,225 sq miles (1,285,216 sq km)
Population: 22,585,000

SURINAME
Capital: Paramaribo
Area: 63,251 sq miles (163,820 sq km)
Population: 405,000

VENEZUELA
Capital: Caracas
Area: 352,145 sq miles (912,050 sq km)
Population: 20,430,000

A B C D E F G H I J K L M N O

13 15 16 17 18 19 20 21 22 23

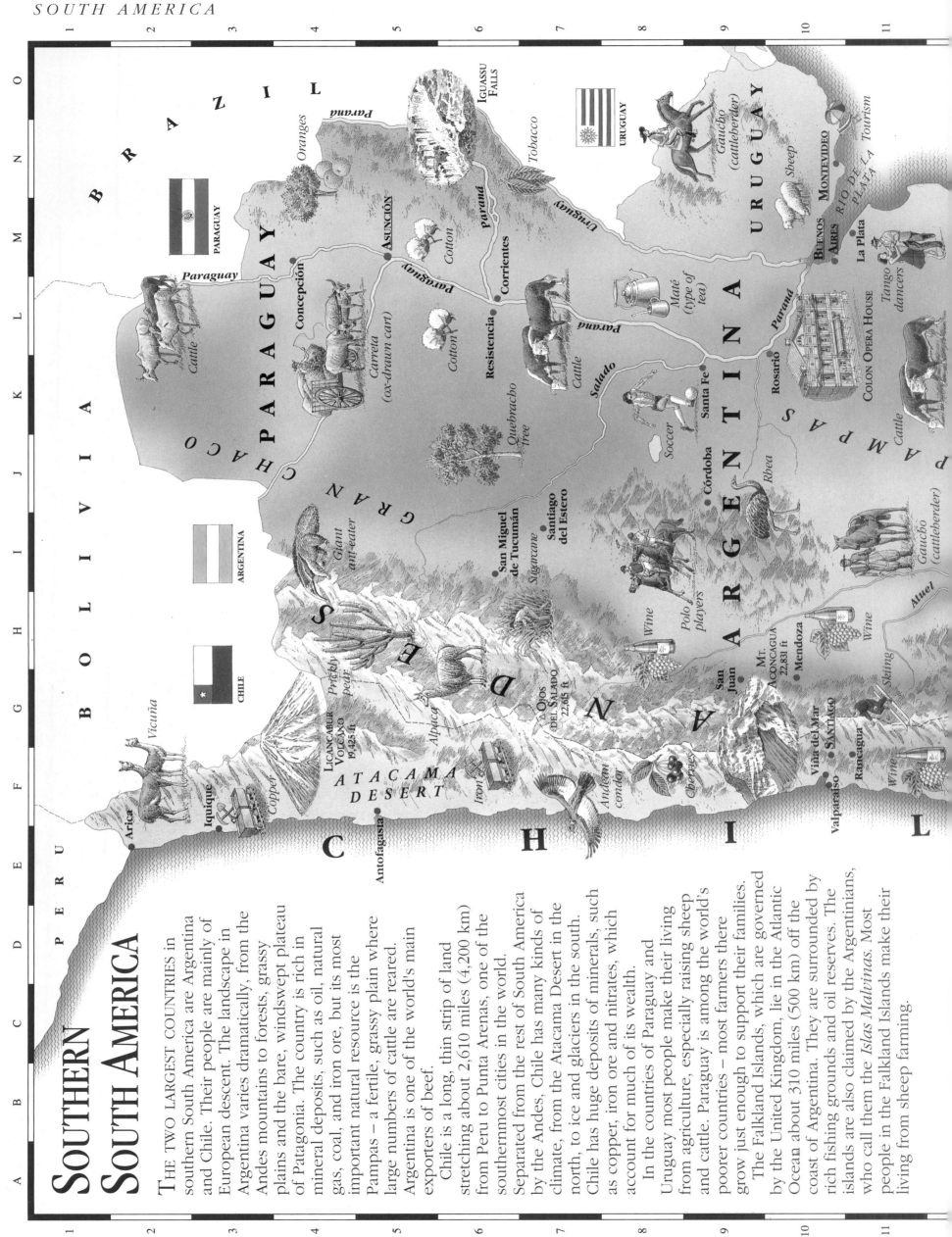

SOUTHERN SOUTH AMERICA

THE TWO LARGEST COUNTRIES in southern South America are Argentina and Chile. Their people are mainly of European descent. The landscape in Argentina varies dramatically, from the Andes mountains to forests, grassy plains and the bare, windswept plateau of Patagonia. The country is rich in mineral deposits, such as oil, natural gas, coal, and iron ore, but its most important natural resource is the Pampas – a fertile, grassy plain where large numbers of cattle are reared. Argentina is one of the world's main exporters of beef.

Chile is a long, thin strip of land stretching about 2,610 miles (4,200 km) from Peru to Punta Arenas, one of the southernmost cities in the world. Separated from the rest of South America by the Andes, Chile has many kinds of climate, from the Atacama Desert in the north, to ice and glaciers in the south. Chile has huge deposits of minerals, such as copper, iron ore and nitrates, which account for much of its wealth.

In the countries of Paraguay and Uruguay most people make their living from agriculture, especially raising sheep and cattle. Paraguay is among the world's poorer countries – most farmers there grow just enough to support their families.

The Falkland Islands, which are governed by the United Kingdom, lie in the Atlantic Ocean about 310 miles (500 km) off the coast of Argentina. They are surrounded by rich fishing grounds and oil reserves. The islands are also claimed by the Argentinians, who call them the *Islas Malvinas*. Most people in the Falkland Islands make their living from sheep farming.

Oranges

Iguassu Falls

Tobacco

PARAGUAY

URUGUAY

Gaucho (cattleherder)

Sheep

MONTEVIDEO

BUENOS AIRES

RÍO DE LA PLATA

La Plata – Tourism

Paraguay

Concepción

ASUNCIÓN

Cotton

Paraná

Corrientes

Resistencia

Cotton

Carreta (ox-drawn cart)

Quebracho tree

Cattle

Maté (type of tea)

Salado

Santa Fe

Rosario

COLON OPERA HOUSE

Tango dancers

P A R A G U A Y

G R A N   C H A C O

B O L I V I A

Soccer

Córdoba

Rhea

A R G E N T I N A

P A M P A S

Cattle

Gaucho (cattleherder)

San Miguel de Tucumán

Santiago del Estero

Sugarcane

Polo players

Wine

Mendoza

Mt. Aconcagua 22,831 ft

San Juan

Wine

Atuel

Giant anteater

Prickly pear

A N D E S

Alpaca

Ojos del Salado 22,615 ft

Andean condor

Cherries

Viña del Mar

SANTIAGO

Skiing

Rancagua

Wine

Vicuña

Arica

Copper

Iquique

LICANCABUR VOLCANO 19,425 ft

A T A C A M A   D E S E R T

Antofagasta

Iron

C H I L E

Valparaíso

P E R U

BRAZIL

Paraná

Paraguay

Paraná

Uruguay

Paraná

Salado

PARAGUAY

ARGENTINA

CHILE

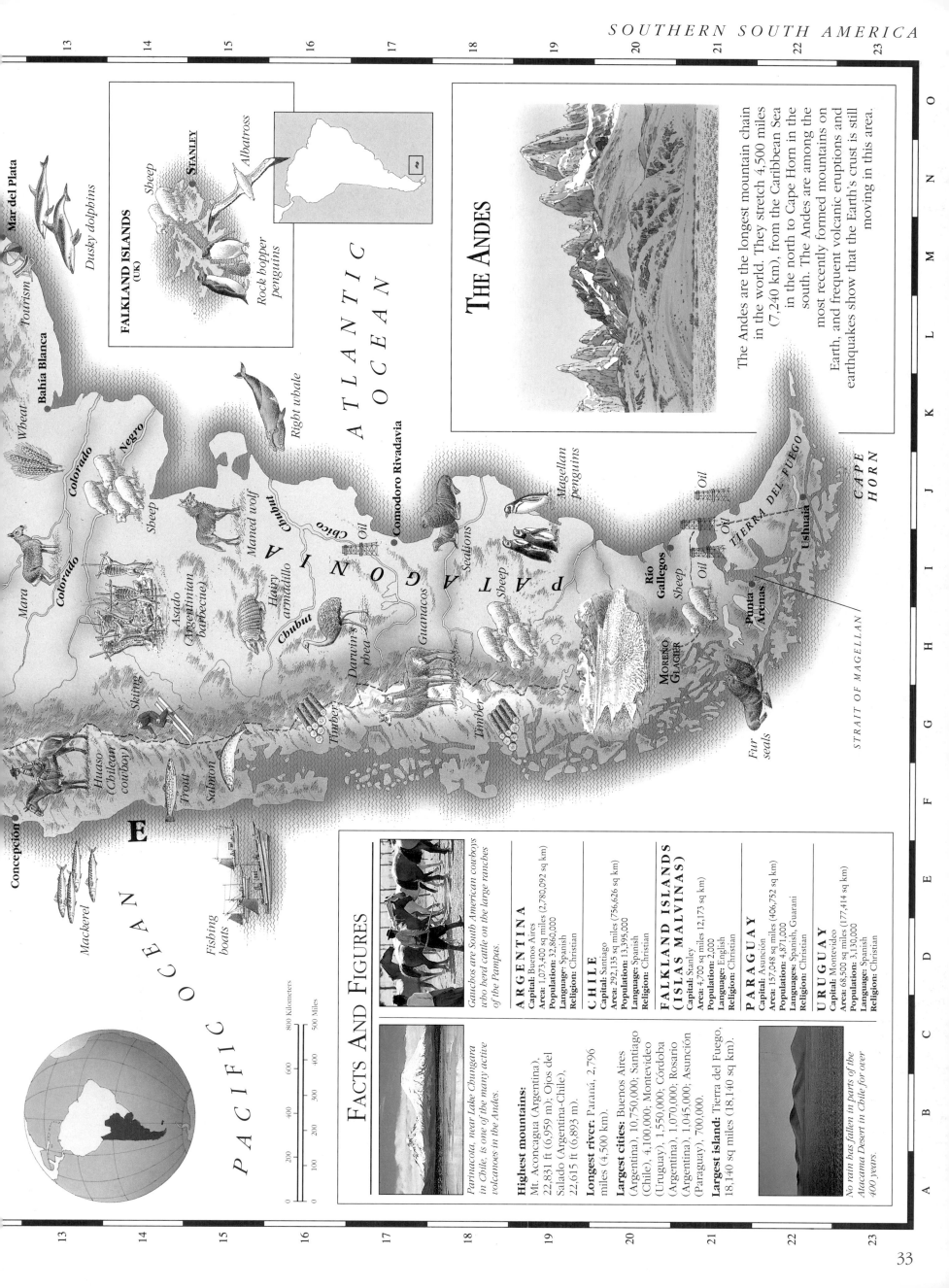

Map labels and features:

Mar del Plata

Dusky dolphins

Tourism

Bahía Blanca

Wheat

Colorado
Negro
Colorado
Colorado

Sheep

Mara

Maned wolf

Chubut

Hairy armadillo

Asado (Argentinian barbecue)

Chubut

Darwin's rhea

Skiing

Huaso (Chilean cowboy)

Trout

Salmon

Timber

Guanacos

Oil

Comodoro Rivadavia

Chico

PATAGONIA

Right whale

ATLANTIC OCEAN

Sea lions

Magellan penguins

Sheep

Timber

Río Gallegos

Sheep

Oil

MORENO GLACIER

Punta Arenas

Oil

Oil

Oil

TIERRA DEL FUEGO

Ushuaia

CAPE HORN

Fur seals

STRAIT OF MAGELLAN

Mackerel

Fishing boats

PACIFIC OCEAN

Concepción

FALKLAND ISLANDS (UK)

Albatross

Sheep

STANLEY

Rock hopper penguins

THE ANDES

The Andes are the longest mountain chain in the world. They stretch 4,500 miles (7,240 km), from the Caribbean Sea in the north to Cape Horn in the south. The Andes are among the most recently formed mountains on Earth, and frequent volcanic eruptions and earthquakes show that the Earth's crust is still moving in this area.

FACTS AND FIGURES

Gauchos are South American cowboys who herd cattle on the large ranches of the Pampas.

ARGENTINA
Capital: Buenos Aires
Area: 1,073,400 sq miles (2,780,092 sq km)
Population: 32,860,000
Language: Spanish
Religion: Christian

CHILE
Capital: Santiago
Area: 292,135 sq miles (756,626 sq km)
Population: 13,395,000
Language: Spanish
Religion: Christian

FALKLAND ISLANDS (ISLAS MALVINAS)
Capital: Stanley
Area: 4,700 sq miles 12,173 sq km)
Population: 2,000
Language: English
Religion: Christian

PARAGUAY
Capital: Asunción
Area: 157,048 sq miles (406,752 sq km)
Population: 4,871,000
Languages: Spanish, Guarani
Religion: Christian

URUGUAY
Capital: Montevideo
Area: 68,500 sq miles (177,414 sq km)
Population: 3,130,000
Language: Spanish
Religion: Christian

Parinacota, near Lake Chungara in Chile, is one of the many active volcanoes in the Andes.

Highest mountains: Mt. Aconcagua (Argentina), 22,831 ft (6,959 m); Ojos del Salado (Argentina-Chile), 22,615 ft (6,893 m).

Longest river: Paraná, 2,796 miles (4,500 km).

Largest cities: Buenos Aires (Argentina), 10,750,000; Santiago (Chile), 4,100,000; Montevideo (Uruguay), 1,550,000; Córdoba (Argentina), 1,070,000; Rosario (Argentina), 1,045,000; Asunción (Paraguay), 700,000.

Largest island: Tierra del Fuego, 18,140 sq miles (18,140 sq km).

No rain has fallen in parts of the Atacama Desert in Chile for over 400 years.

800 Kilometers
500 Miles

EUROPE

The headquarters of the EC in Brussels, Belgium.

EUROPE IS THE SECOND smallest continent in terms of area, but it has the second largest population of all the seven continents. Europe is bounded by the Atlantic and Arctic Oceans in the north and west, and in the south by the Mediterranean Sea. Europe's only land frontier – with Asia – is marked by the Ural and Caucasus mountains in Russia.

The landscape of Europe is greatly varied. In southern Europe, much of the land is hilly or mountainous. The history of this region has been greatly influenced by the Mediterranean Sea, which for centuries has been a vital trade route between Europe, Africa, and Asia.

The northern and southern parts of mainland Europe are divided by the Alps, the highest range of mountains in western Europe. The landscape of northern Europe is generally flat and is dominated by the North European Plain, which stretches from the Atlantic coast right across to the Ural Mountains. In the far north of the continent lie the mainly mountainous countries of Scandinavia.

In 1945, after the end of the Second World War, the European countries were divided into two groups – the West and East. The border between them was sometimes described as an Iron Curtain, because few people were allowed to cross it.

The Eastern European countries were Romania, Poland, Yugoslavia, Czechoslovakia, Hungary, Bulgaria, Albania, and the area that was formerly East Germany. Until the late 1980s, these countries had communist governments, and many of them were closely linked to the former USSR. But in recent years, almost all the

Vegetable market in Montenegro, Yugoslavia.

Eastern European countries have abandoned communism and relations between them and Western Europe have improved. Today, Eastern Europe also includes the three Baltic States – Latvia, Lithuania, and Estonia – along with Belarus, Ukraine, and Moldova, all of which were formerly part of the USSR, and Croatia, Slovenia, Bosnia and Herzegovina, and Macedonia, which split away from Yugoslavia in 1992. In 1993 Czechoslovakia split into two countries – the Czech Republic and Slovakia.

The Western European nations are among the richest in the world. Twelve countries in Western Europe have joined together to form the European Community (EC). The member states are Belgium, Denmark, France, Germany, Greece, Ireland, Italy, Luxembourg, the Netherlands, Spain, Portugal, and the UK. The aim of the EC is to unite the economic resources of its members into a single economy. In the future, there may also be a form of political union.

In the 18th and 19th centuries, Western European countries became the first nations in the world to have an industrial revolution. They changed from farming to the manufacture and export of industrial goods. Today Europe has the greatest concentration of industry of all the continents, but many Europeans still make their living from farming.

Lavender fields in France.

FACTS ABOUT EUROPE

Area: 4,053,309 sq miles (10,498,000 sq km). This is seven percent of the world's total land area.

Population: 690,000,000 (including the European part of Russia). This is nearly 14 percent of the world's total population.

Number of countries: 42 (this includes 3 percent of Turkey and 25 percent of Russia).

Largest countries: Russia – the European part of Russia covers 1,527,350 sq miles (3,955,818 sq km), this is only 23 percent of the total area of Russia; France, 211,208 sq miles (547,026 sq km).

Most populated countries: Russia – 109,930,000 people live in the European part of Russia; Germany, 79,710,000.

Largest cities: Moscow (Russia), 13,150,000; London (UK), 11,100,000; Paris (France), 10,275,000; St. Petersburg (Russia), 5,525,000; Essen (Germany), 5,050,000.

Highest mountains: Mt. Elbrus (Russia), 18,510 ft (5,642 m); Mont Blanc (France-Italy), 15,771 ft (4,807 m); Monte Rosa (Italy-Switzerland), 15,203 ft (4,634 m).

Longest rivers: Volga, 2,194 miles (3,531 km); Danube, 1,776 miles (2,858 km); Dnieper, 1,368 miles (2,201 km).

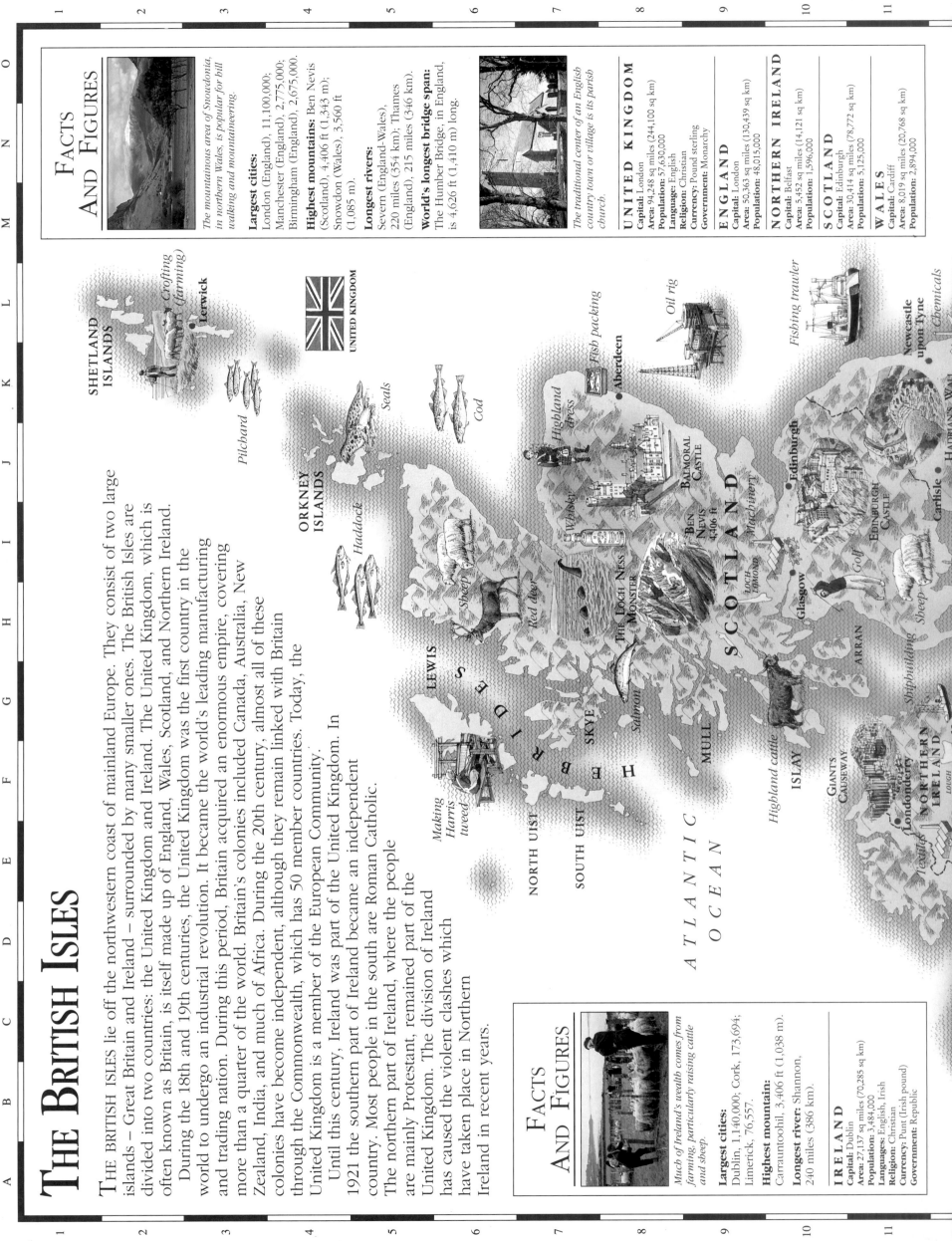

THE BRITISH ISLES

THE BRITISH ISLES lie off the northwestern coast of mainland Europe. They consist of two large islands – Great Britain and Ireland – surrounded by many smaller ones. The British Isles are divided into two countries: the United Kingdom and Ireland. The United Kingdom, which is often known as Britain, is itself made up of England, Wales, Scotland, and Northern Ireland.

During the 18th and 19th centuries, the United Kingdom was the first country in the world to undergo an industrial revolution. It became the world's leading manufacturing and trading nation. During this period, Britain acquired an enormous empire, covering more than a quarter of the world. Britain's colonies included Canada, Australia, New Zealand, India, and much of Africa. During the 20th century, almost all of these colonies have become independent, although they remain linked with Britain through the Commonwealth, which has 50 member countries. Today, the United Kingdom is a member of the European Community.

Until this century, Ireland was part of the United Kingdom. In 1921 the southern part of Ireland became an independent country. Most people in the south are Roman Catholic. The northern part of Ireland, where the people are mainly Protestant, remained part of the United Kingdom. The division of Ireland has caused the violent clashes which have taken place in Northern Ireland in recent years.

FACTS AND FIGURES

The mountainous area of Snowdonia, in northern Wales, is popular for hill walking and mountaineering.

Largest cities:
London (England), 11,100,000;
Manchester (England), 2,775,000;
Birmingham (England), 2,675,000.

Highest mountains: Ben Nevis (Scotland), 4,406 ft (1,343 m); Snowdon (Wales), 3,560 ft (1,085 m).

Longest rivers:
Severn (England-Wales), 220 miles (354 km); Thames (England), 215 miles (346 km).

World's longest bridge span:
The Humber Bridge, in England, is 4,626 ft (1,410 m) long.

The traditional center of an English country town or village is its parish church.

UNITED KINGDOM
Capital: London
Area: 94,248 sq miles (244,100 sq km)
Population: 57,630,000
Language: English
Religion: Christian
Currency: Pound sterling
Government: Monarchy

ENGLAND
Capital: London
Area: 50,363 sq miles (130,439 sq km)
Population: 48,015,000

NORTHERN IRELAND
Capital: Belfast
Area: 5,452 sq miles (14,121 sq km)
Population: 1,596,000

SCOTLAND
Capital: Edinburgh
Area: 30,414 sq miles (78,772 sq km)
Population: 5,125,000

WALES
Capital: Cardiff
Area: 8,019 sq miles (20,768 sq km)
Population: 2,894,000

FACTS AND FIGURES

Much of Ireland's wealth comes from farming, particularly raising cattle and sheep.

Largest cities:
Dublin, 1,140,000; Cork, 173,694; Limerick, 76,557.

Highest mountain:
Carrauntoohil, 3,406 ft (1,038 m).

Longest river: Shannon, 240 miles (386 km).

IRELAND
Capital: Dublin
Area: 27,137 sq miles (70,285 sq km)
Population: 3,484,000
Languages: English, Irish
Religion: Christian
Currency: Punt (Irish pound)
Government: Republic

UNITED KINGDOM

SHETLAND ISLANDS

Crofting (farming)

Lerwick

Pilchard

Seals

Cod

ORKNEY ISLANDS

Haddock

HEBRIDES

LEWIS

SKYE

NORTH UIST

SOUTH UIST

Making Harris tweed

Sheep

Red deer

Salmon

MULL

ISLAY

ARRAN

ATLANTIC OCEAN

Highland dress

Aberdeen

Oil rig

Fish packing

Whisky

Macbuter

BEN NEVIS 4,406 ft

THE LOCH NESS MONSTER

LOCH LOMOND

SCOTLAND

BALMORAL CASTLE

Glasgow

Edinburgh

EDINBURGH CASTLE

Golf

Sheep

Carlisle

HADRIAN'S WALL

Newcastle upon Tyne

Chemicals

Fishing trawler

Shipbuilding

GIANTS CAUSEWAY

Highland cattle

Londonderry

NORTHERN IRELAND

LOUGH

Textiles

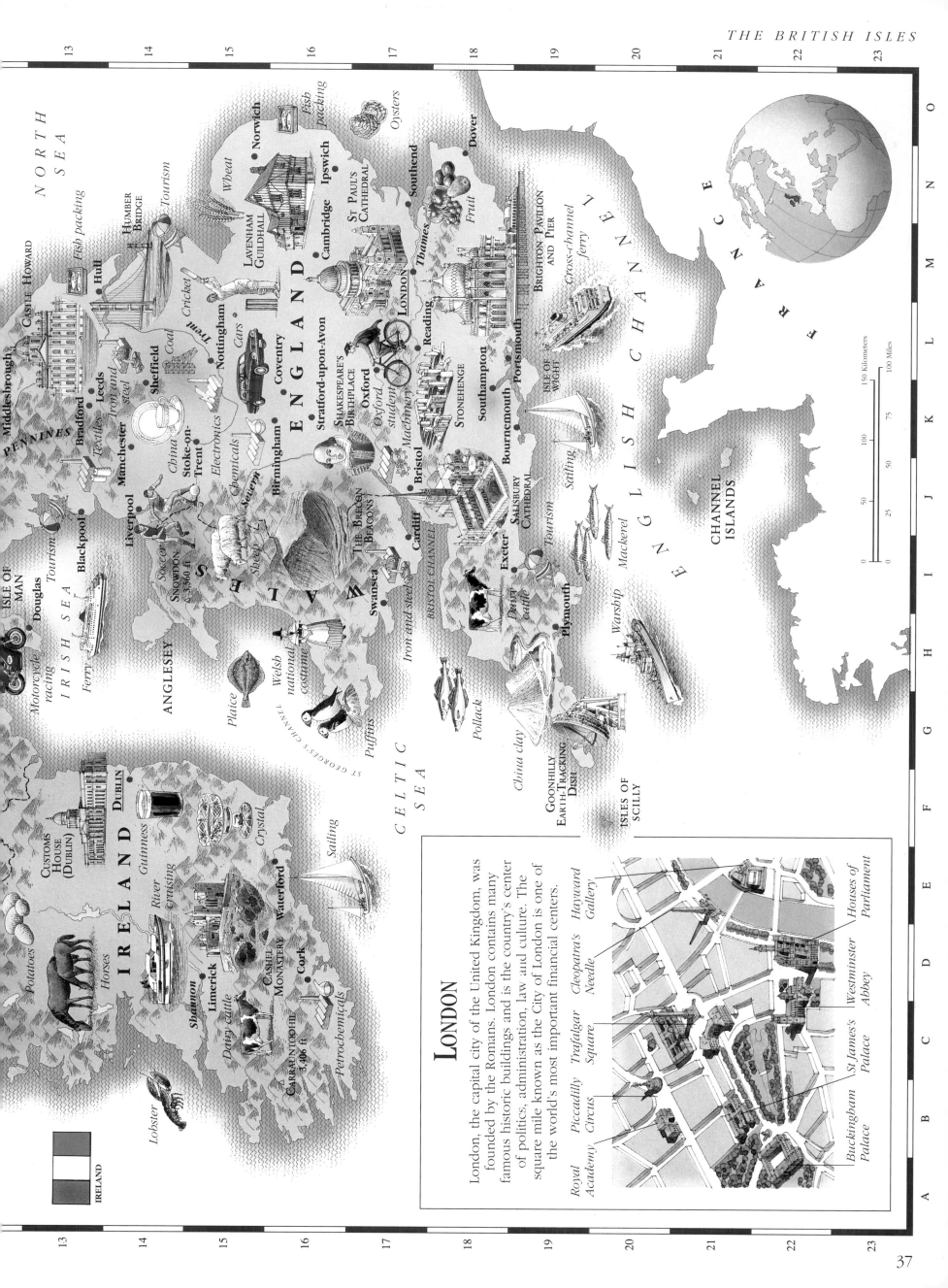

NORTH SEA

IRISH SEA

CELTIC SEA

ST GEORGE'S CHANNEL

BRISTOL CHANNEL

ENGLISH CHANNEL

FRANCE

IRELAND

CUSTOMS HOUSE (DUBLIN)
DUBLIN

River cruising
Guinness
Crystal
Sailing

Limerick
Shannon
Dairy cattle
CASHEL MONASTERY
Waterford
Cork
Petrochemicals
CARRAUNTOOHIL 3,406 ft
Horses
Potatoes
Lobster

Middlesbrough
CASTLE HOWARD
Fish packing
Hull
HUMBER BRIDGE
Tourism

PENNINES
Bradford
Leeds
Textiles
Iron and steel
Sheffield
Coal
Trent
Cricket

ISLE OF MAN
Douglas
Motorcycle racing
Tourism
Blackpool
Soccer

Liverpool
Manchester
China
Stoke-on-Trent
Electronics
Chemicals
Birmingham
Coventry
Cars
Nottingham

ANGLESEY

SNOWDON 3,560 ft
Sheep
Welsh national costume
Plaice
Puffins

W A L E S
THE BRECON BEACONS
Swansea
Cardiff
Iron and steel
Severn
Stratford-upon-Avon
SHAKESPEARE'S BIRTHPLACE
Oxford
OXFORD STUDENT

E N G L A N D

Wheat
Norwich
Fish packing
FISH
LAVENHAM GUILDHALL
Cambridge
Ipswich
ST PAUL'S CATHEDRAL
Oysters

Thames
LONDON
Reading
Southend
Dover
Fruit

Bristol
Machinery
Dairy cattle
Exeter
Tourism
Pollack
China clay
GOONHILLY EARTH-TRACKING DISH
ISLES OF SCILLY
Plymouth
Warship

SALISBURY CATHEDRAL
STONEHENGE
Southampton
Bournemouth
Portsmouth
ISLE OF WIGHT
Sailing
Mackerel

BRIGHTON PAVILION AND PIER
Cross-channel ferry

CHANNEL ISLANDS

150 Kilometers
100 Miles
0 25 50 75 100
0 50 100

IRELAND

LONDON

London, the capital city of the United Kingdom, was founded by the Romans. London contains many famous historic buildings and is the country's center of politics, administration, law and culture. The square mile known as the City of London is one of the world's most important financial centers.

Royal Academy
Piccadilly Circus
Trafalgar Square
Cleopatra's Needle
Hayward Gallery
Houses of Parliament
Westminster Abbey
St James's Palace
Buckingham Palace

FRANCE

FRANCE is one of Europe's major farming and industrial nations and is famous for the food and wine it produces. The landscape in France varies dramatically from region to region and includes rich farmland; hot, dry areas; snow-capped mountains; and large forests.

France has always been an important European power. In 1789 the French overthrew their king, Louis XVI, during the French Revolution. After the revolution, Napoleon, a general in the French army, seized power and crowned himself Emperor. He went on to conquer most of mainland Europe, but was defeated at the Battle of Waterloo in 1815. During the 19th century, French explorers and soldiers won a large colonial empire in Africa and Asia.

Today France is one of the world's leading manufacturing countries, with large iron, steel, chemical, car, airplane, and textile industries. France is also rich in farming land. Its major crops include barley, oats, wheat, flax, sugarbeet, and grapes. Dairy farming is widespread and French farmers produce over 700 different types of cheese.

Tourism is another important source of wealth. There are many resorts around the coasts of France, and the Alps and Pyrenees are popular for winter sports.

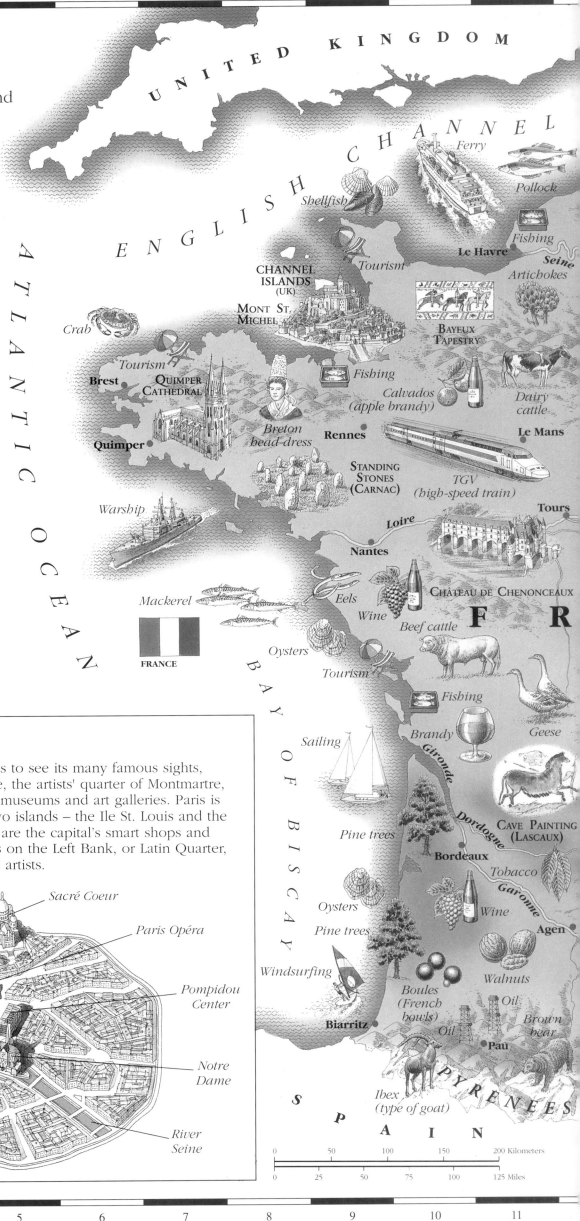

PARIS

Visitors from all over the world flock to Paris to see its many famous sights, including the Eiffel Tower, the Arc de Triomphe, the artists' quarter of Montmartre, the tree-lined avenues, or *boulevards,* and the museums and art galleries. Paris is built on both sides of the River Seine and on two islands – the Ile St. Louis and the Ile de la Cité. On the Right Bank of the river are the capital's smart shops and fashion houses. The many cafés and bookshops on the Left Bank, or Latin Quarter, attract students and artists.

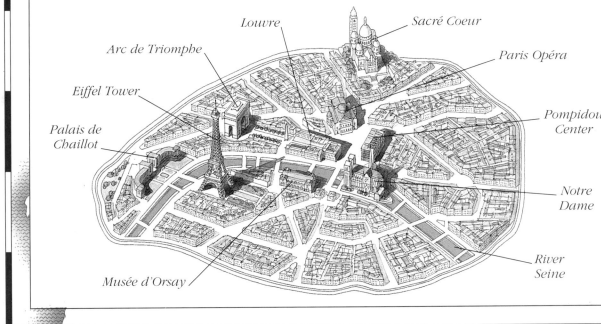

BELGIUM

Calais
Dunkerque
Lille

Tourism

Somme

Amiens

AMIENS CATHEDRAL

WORLD WAR I MEMORIAL (VIMY)

Beef cattle

Fashion design

Cars

PARIS

CHÂTEAU DE PIERREFONDS

Wheat

Seine

CHARTRES CATHEDRAL

Orléans

Loire

CHÂTEAU DE CHAMBORD

CHÂTEAU BAS (SEDAN)

Reims

Champagne

Wild boar

SAINTE MADELEINE (VÉZELAY)

Mustard

Wine

CHÂTEAUNEUF (NIÈVRE)

Potatoes

Nancy

Pigs

Dijon

Beaune

Saône

Wine

Mâcon

Metz

LUXEMBOURG

Coal

Coal

GERMANY

Wine

Strasbourg

Storks

Mulhouse

CHAPEL OF NOTRE DAME DU HAUT

VOSGES

JURA

SWITZERLAND

Deer

F R A N C E

Porcelain

Limoges

Hunting for truffles

Clermont-Ferrand

MASSIF CENTRAL

Cycling

CHAPEL OF ST. MICHEL D'AIGUILHE (LE PUY)

TGV (high-speed train)

St. Etienne

Lyon

Skiing

Grenoble

Mountain climbing

Chamois (type of goat)

A L P S

C E V E N N E S

Rhône

Wine

Olives

Sheep

Tourism

PONT VALENTRE (CAHORS)

Garonne

Snails

Aircraft industry

Montpellier

Toulouse

WALLED TOWN (CARCASSONNE)

AMPHITHEATER AT ARLES

Lavender

Flamingos

Sailing

Fishing

Warship

Marseille

Toulon

Tourism

Tourism

MONT BLANC 15,770 ft

I T A L Y

MONACO

Nice

Cannes

Tourism

S E A

Tourism

SOLAR FURNACE (ODEILLO)

Wine

Sardines

M E D I T E R R A N E A N

MONACO

FACTS AND FIGURES

Amboise is one of the many historic towns situated along the River Loire in western France.

Highest mountains:
Mont Blanc, 15,771 ft (4,807 m); Les Ecrins, 13,461 ft (4,103 m); Pic de Vignemale, 10,820 ft (3,298 m); Mont Dore, 6,188 ft (1,886 m).

Longest rivers:
Loire, 625 miles (1,005 km); Rhône-Saône, 505 miles (812 km); Seine, 481 miles (775 km).

Largest cities:
Paris, 10,275,000; Lyon, 1,335,000; Marseille, 1,225,000; Lille, 1,050,000; Bordeaux, 760,000.

The TGV, which runs between Paris and Lyon, is one of the world's fastest trains, with a top speed of 168 mph (270 kph).

FRANCE
Capital: Paris
Area: 212,208 sq miles (547,026 sq km)
Population: 57,010,000
Language: French
Religion: Christian
Currency: French franc

MONACO
Capital: Monaco
Area: 0.7 sq miles (1.9 sq km)
Population: 30,000
Language: French
Religion: Christian
Currency: French franc

Sunflowers are grown all over southern France. Their seeds are used to make cooking oil.

CORSICA (FRANCE)

Bastia

Tourism

Ajaccio

Tourism

CORSICA

BELGIUM, THE NETHERLANDS, AND LUXEMBOURG

BELGIUM, THE NETHERLANDS, AND LUXEMBOURG are situated on the North European Plain, where much of the land is very flat and low lying. For this reason, they are often called the "Low Countries". The only area of higher land in the region is the hilly Ardennes forest in southern Belgium and Luxembourg.

Almost half of the Netherlands lies below sea level. There is a saying that "God made the world, but the Dutch made the Netherlands", because over the centuries the Dutch have reclaimed large areas of land from the sea. The reclaimed land, called a polder, is drained and then protected against flooding with long walls called dikes.

Belgium, the Netherlands, and Luxembourg are sometimes called "Benelux", which is a shortened version of the three country names. Although these countries are small, they have large populations. The Netherlands has one of the highest concentrations of people in Europe – an average of 936 people live in each square mile of land.

All three Benelux countries have successful industrial economies. Farming is also important, and the most up-to-date methods are used. The main products are livestock, dairy products, fruit, vegetables, and flowers. Fishing and tourism are also important sources of income. Today, Belgium and the Netherlands have been important trading nations for many centuries. Today, Rotterdam in the Netherlands and Antwerp in Belgium are the two busiest ports in Europe.

The Benelux countries are members of the European Community, which has its headquarters in Brussels, the Belgian capital. Luxembourg is a center for European organizations, while the International Courts of Justice are situated at The Hague in the Netherlands.

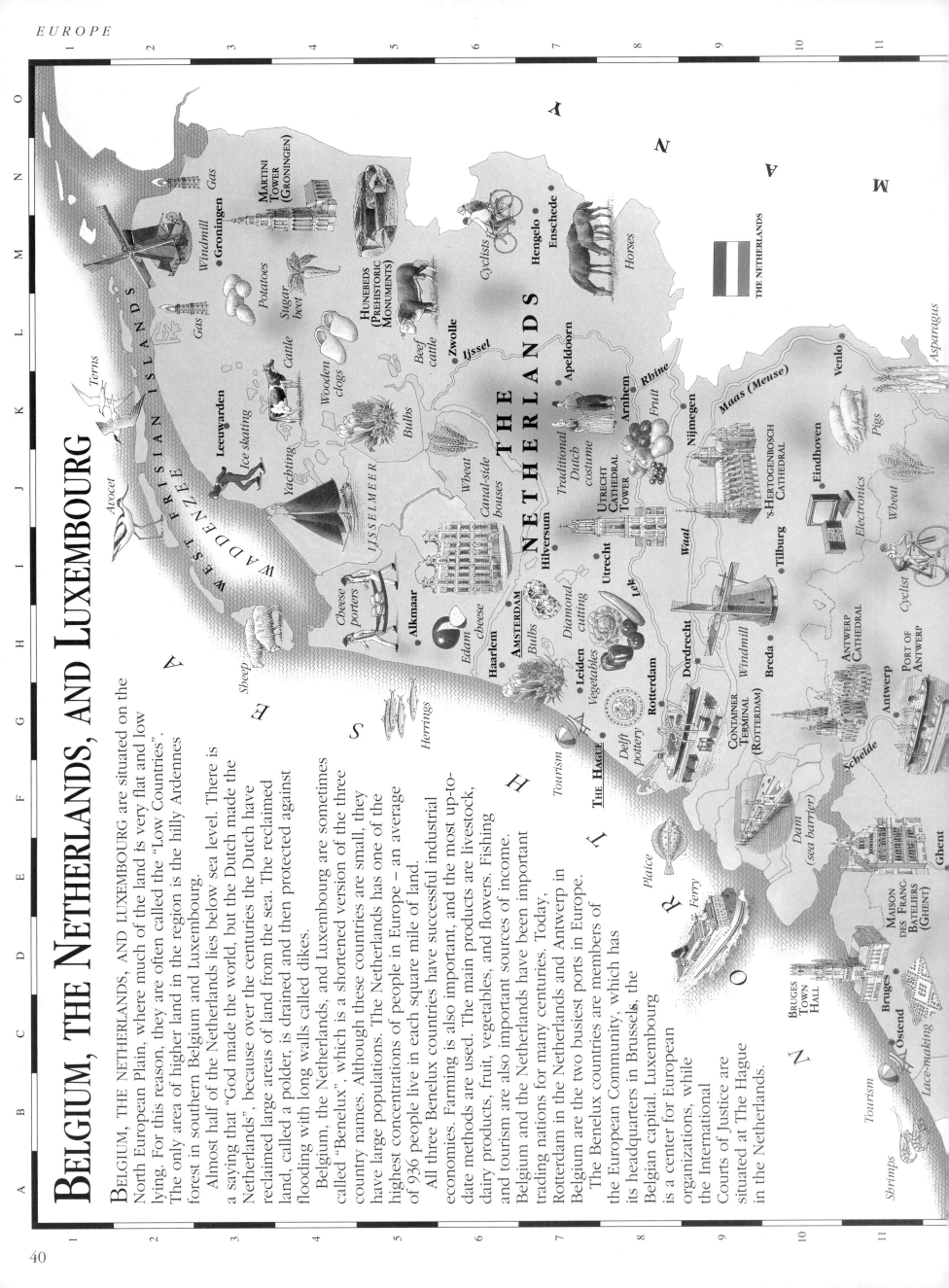

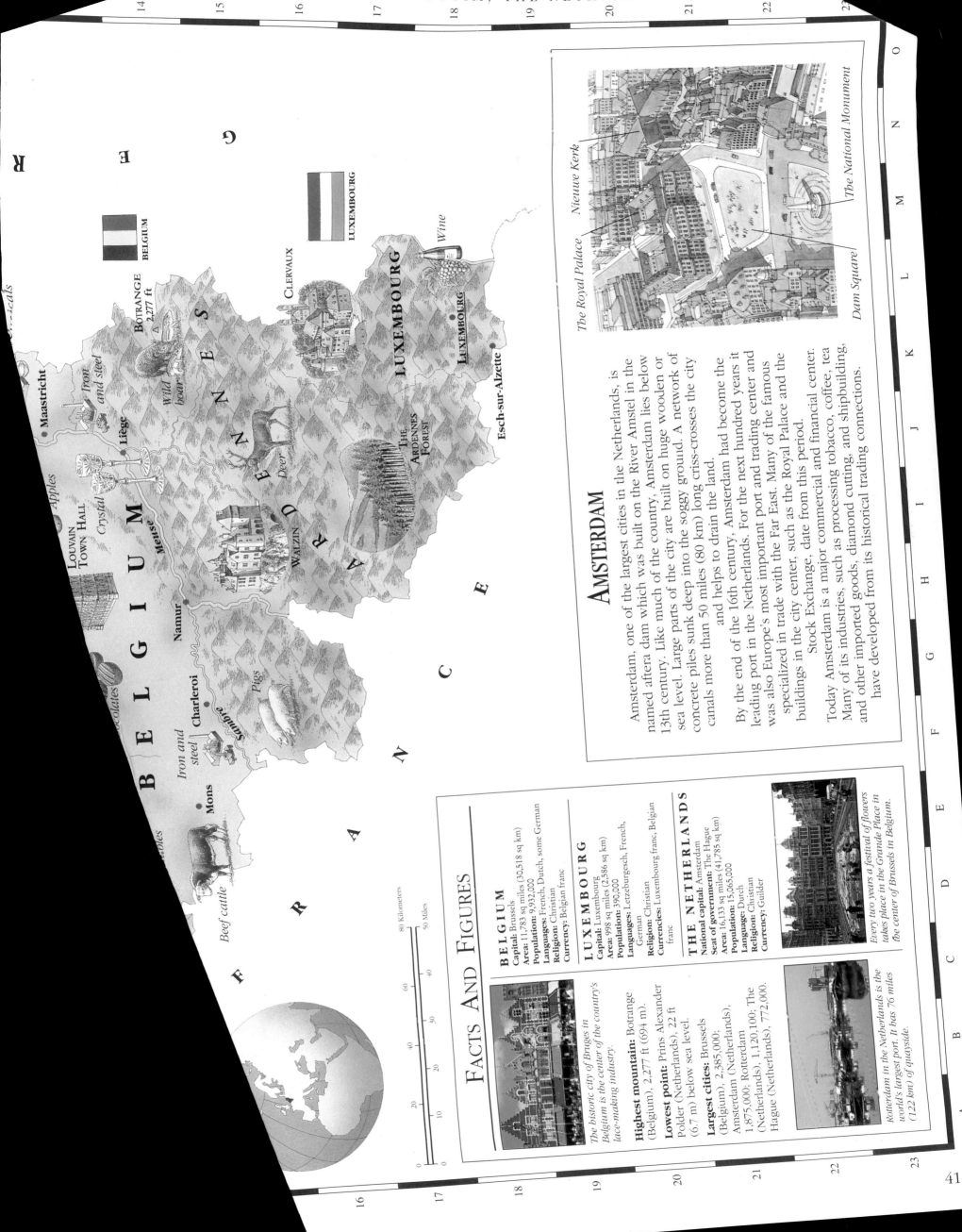

The Royal Palace — *Nieuwe Kerk* — *The National Monument* — *Dam Square*

AMSTERDAM

Amsterdam, one of the largest cities in the Netherlands, is named after a dam which was built on the River Amstel in the 13th century. Like much of the country, Amsterdam lies below sea level. Large parts of the city are built on huge woolen or concrete piles sunk deep into the soggy ground. A network of canals more than 50 miles (80 km) long criss-crosses the city and helps to drain the land.

By the end of the 16th century, Amsterdam had become the leading port in the Netherlands. For the next hundred years it was also Europe's most important port and trading center and specialized in trade with the Far East. Many of the famous buildings in the city center, such as the Royal Palace and the Stock Exchange, date from this period.

Today Amsterdam is a major commercial and financial center. Many of its industries, such as processing tobacco, coffee, tea and other imported goods, diamond cutting, and shipbuilding, have developed from its historical trading connections.

FACTS AND FIGURES

BELGIUM
Capital: Brussels
Area: 11,783 sq miles (30,518 sq km)
Population: 9,932,000
Languages: French, Dutch, some German
Religion: Christian
Currency: Belgian franc

LUXEMBOURG
Capital: Luxembourg
Area: 998 sq miles (2,586 sq km)
Population: 390,000
Languages: Letzeburgesch, French, German
Religion: Christian
Currencies: Luxembourg franc, Belgian franc

THE NETHERLANDS
National capital: Amsterdam
Seat of government: The Hague
Area: 16,133 sq miles (41,785 sq km)
Population: 15,065,000
Language: Dutch
Religion: Christian
Currency: Guilder

Every two years a festival of flowers takes place in the Grande Place in the center of Brussels in Belgium.

Highest mountain: Botrange (Belgium), 2,277 ft (694 m).
Lowest point: Prins Alexander Polder (Netherlands), 22 ft (6.7 m) below sea level.
Largest cities: Brussels (Belgium), 2,385,000; Amsterdam (Netherlands), 1,875,000; Rotterdam (Netherlands), 1,120,100; The Hague (Netherlands), 772,000.

The historic city of Bruges in Belgium is the center of the country's lace-making industry.

Rotterdam in the Netherlands is the world's largest port. It has 76 miles (122 km) of quayside.

80 Kilometers
50 Miles

Map labels

BELGIUM
LUXEMBOURG
Maastricht
Liège
Louvain Town Hall
Namur
Charleroi
Mons
Sambre
Meuse
Pigs
Apples
Crystal
Iron and steel
Beef cattle
Chocolates
Wild boar
Deer
Iron and steel
Botrange 2,277 ft
Clervaux
Walzin
THE ARDENNES FOREST
ARDENNES
Luxembourg
Esch-sur-Alzette
Wine

FRANCE
GERMANY

BELGIUM
LUXEMBOURG

SCANDINAVIA

SCANDINAVIA consists of the four countries of Denmark, Norway, Sweden, and Finland, which are situated in northern Europe, and the island of Iceland, which lies in the North Atlantic Ocean.

The landscape of Scandinavia varies from country to country. Denmark is low lying, and much of the land is used for farming. In contrast, almost all of Norway is mountainous, and the country's coastline is dotted with long, narrow bays called fjords. Finland is a land of forests and lakes, while Sweden has an extremely varied landscape, which includes forest, farmland, mountains,

and lakes. The central part of Iceland is a plateau of volcanoes, lava fields and glaciers, so most of the people live around the coast. The people of Scandinavia are the descendants of the Vikings, who lived there about 1,000 years ago. The Vikings are usually remembered as warriors and seafarers, but for most of the time they lived peacefully as farmers and fishermen.

Scandinavia has important natural resources, including the timber in its large forests, fish in the surrounding seas, iron ore in northern Sweden, and oil and natural gas in the North Sea off the coast of Norway. Today, the Scandinavian countries all have successful industrial economies, and their people enjoy a high standard of living.

THE FJORDS

During the last great Ice Age, huge ice sheets and glaciers formed over Scandinavia. The moving ice carved out deep, steep-sided valleys. When the ice sheets began to melt, about 11,000 years ago, many of these valleys were filled by the sea, forming the famous Norwegian fjords.

ICELAND

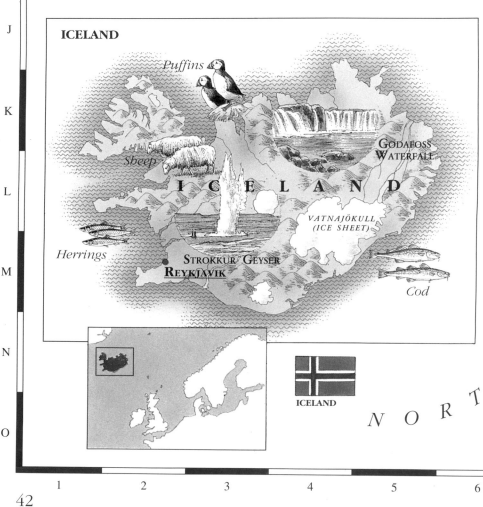

Puffins

GODAFOSS WATERFALL

Sheep

I C E L A N D

VATNAJÖKULL (ICE SHEET)

Herrings

STROKKUR GEYSER
REYKJAVIK

Cod

ICELAND

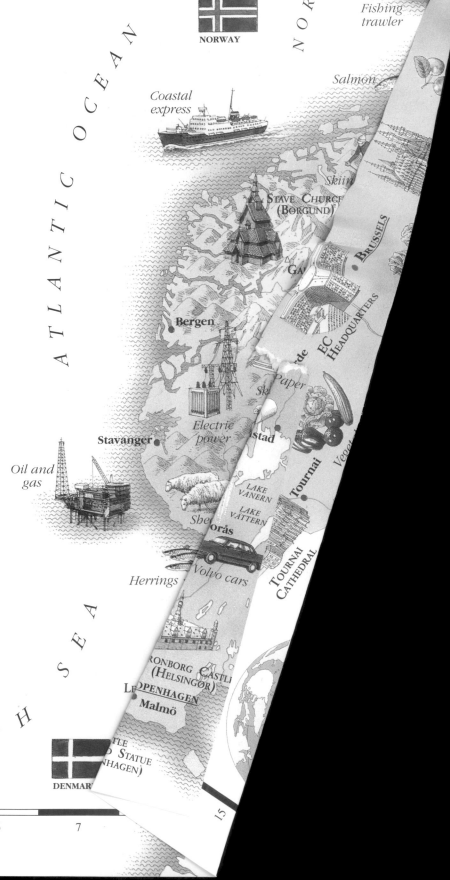

NORWEGIAN SEA

Fishing trawler

NORWAY

Salmon

Coastal express

ATLANTIC OCEAN

STAVE CHURCH (BORGUND)

BRUSSELS

EC HEADQUARTERS

Bergen

Paper

Electric power

Stavanger

Oil and gas

Tournai

LAKE VANERN
LAKE VÄTTERN

Herrings

Volvo cars

TOURNAI CATHEDRAL

NORTH SEA

RONBORG CASTLE (HELSINGØR)
OPENHAGEN
Malmö

STATUE
HAGEN)

DENMARK

13 14 15 19 20 21 22 23

A
B
C
D
E
F
G
H
I
J
K
L
M
N
O

BARENTS
SEA

*Fishing
trawler*

Cod

Tromsø

Reindeer

Puffins

Narvik

*Sami
(Lapps)*

LOFOTEN
ISLANDS

N O R W A Y

L A P L A N D

Iron ore

Wolves

Salmon

*Birch
tree*

Elk

Lynx

S W E D E N

F I N L A N D

*Cross-
country
skiing*

Sailing

Oulu

Sauna

*Norway
spruce*

Furs

Umeå

G U L F   O F   B O T H N I A

*Scots
pine*

Salmon

*Folk
costume*

Herrings

**TAMPERE
CATHEDRAL**

Paper

Trout

*Model horse
(Dalarna)*

Tampere

**DROTTINGHOLM
PALACE**

Lahti

Potatoes

**HELSINKI
RAILWAY
STATION**

Turku

HELSINKI

Uppsala

ÅLAND
ISLANDS

G U L F   O F   F I N L A N D

Örebro

STOCKHOLM

*Ice-breaker
ship*

**CITY HALL
(STOCKHOLM)**

E S T O N I A

*Rune stone
(ancient
inscription)*

GOTLAND

B A L T I C   S E A

ÖLAND

Guillemots

L A T V I A

SWEDEN

R U S S I A

FINLAND

FACTS
AND FIGURES

*Scandinavia's large forests are an
important source of wealth. Much of
the timber is used to make paper.*

Highest mountain:
Galdhøpiggen (Norway), 8,100 ft
(2,469 m).

Largest lake: Lake Vänern
(Sweden), 2,155 sq miles
(5,580 sq km).

Largest cities:
Copenhagen (Denmark),
1,685,000; Stockholm (Sweden),
1,449,972; Helsinki (Finland),
1,040,000; Oslo (Norway),
720,000; Göteborg (Sweden),
710,894.

*The city of Copenhagen in Denmark
has been an important port and
trading center since the Middle Ages.*

DENMARK
Capital: Copenhagen
Area: 16,638 sq miles (43,093 sq km)
Population: 5,154,000
Language: Danish
Religion: Christian
Currency: Danish krone
Government: Monarchy

FINLAND
Capital: Helsinki
Area: 130,559 sq miles (338,145 sq km)
Population: 5,001,000
Languages: Finnish, Swedish, Lappish
Religion: Christian
Currency: Markka
Government: Republic

ICELAND
Capital: Reykjavik
Area: 39,769 sq miles (103,000 sq km)
Population: 261,000
Language: Icelandic
Religion: Christian
Currency: Icelandic krona
Government: Republic

NORWAY
Capital: Oslo
Area: 149,412 sq miles (386,975 sq km)
Population: 4,286,000
Languages: Norwegian, Lappish
Religion: Christian
Currency: Norwegian krone
Government: Monarchy

SWEDEN
Capital: Stockholm
Area: 173,732 sq miles (449,964 sq km)
Population: 8,581,000
Language: Swedish, Lappish
Religion: Christian
Currency: Swedish krona
Government: Monarchy

*In central Iceland, volcanoes and hot
water springs lie next to frozen rivers
of ice, called glaciers.*

0   50   100   150   200   250 Kilometers

0   50   100   150 Miles

13 14 15 16 17 18 19 20 21 22 23

GERMANY, AUSTRIA, AND SWITZERLAND

THE LANDSCAPE in this region varies greatly, changing from flat plains in the north to high mountains in the south. It is crossed by two of Europe's longest rivers: the Rhine, which flows northwards to the North Sea, and the Danube, which flows eastwards to the Black Sea.

For hundreds of years, the area now called Germany consisted of many small independent states. These states were first united to form a single country in 1871. Germany rapidly became an important industrial and political power. In this century, Germany was defeated in two world wars. After World War II the country was split into two parts: the Federal Republic of Germany (West Germany) and the communist German Democratic Republic (East Germany). This split lasted for over 40 years. During this period relations between the two countries were often hostile because of their different political systems. The two German states were reunited in 1990, following the collapse of the communist government in East Germany. Today, Germany is among the world's most successful industrial nations and is the wealthiest country in Europe.

South of Germany lie the mountainous countries of Austria and Switzerland. Tourism, particularly winter sports, is an important source of wealth for both these countries. Switzerland is famous for its watches and scientific instruments, and is also a major banking and business center. The country has been neutral since 1815 and has stayed out of all the wars that have affected Europe since that time. Austria is also neutral. The tiny country of Liechtenstein, which lies between Switzerland and Austria, is only about 15 miles (24 km) long and 5 miles (8 km) wide.

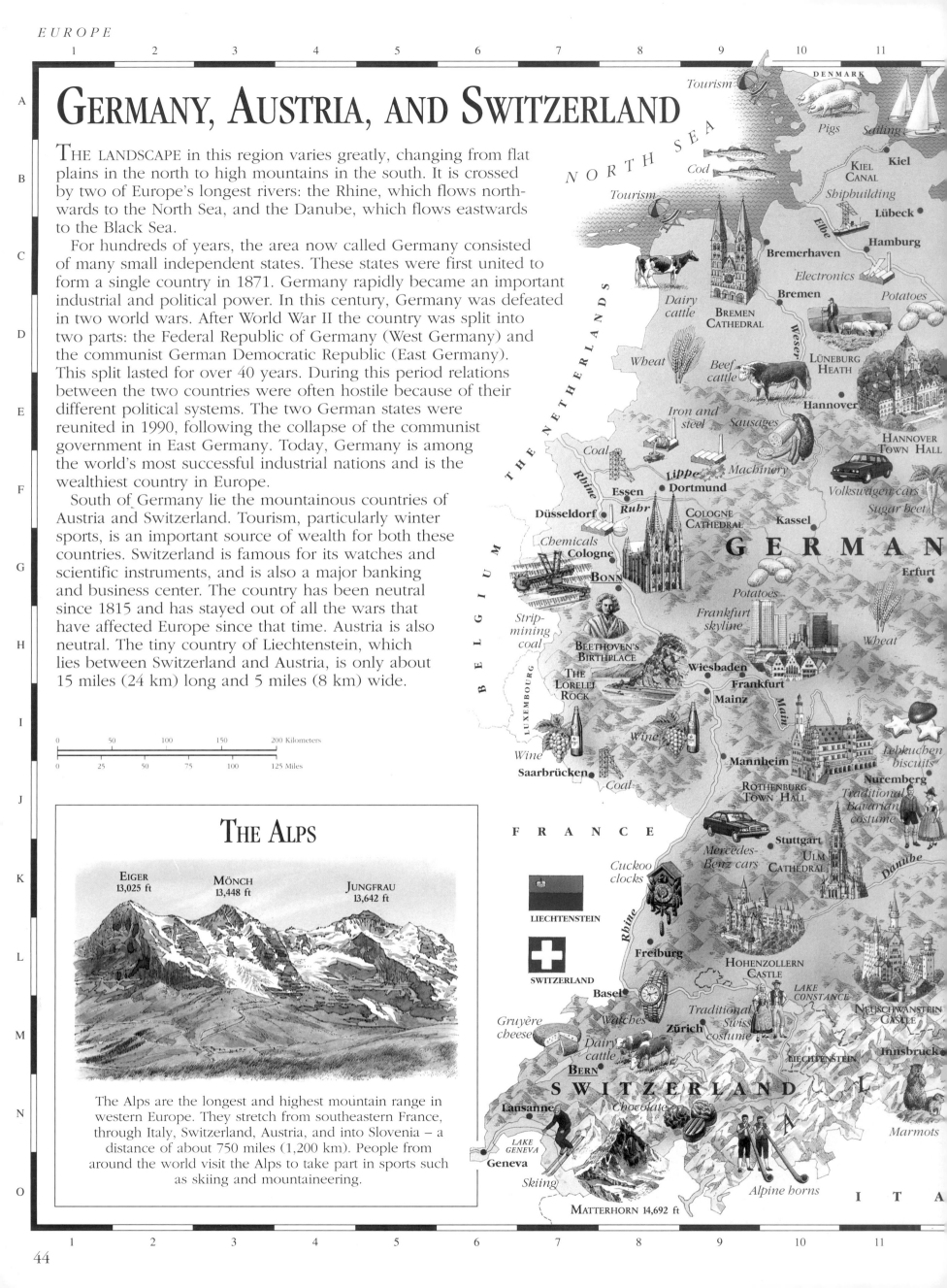

THE ALPS

EIGER 13,025 ft MÖNCH 13,448 ft JUNGFRAU 13,642 ft

The Alps are the longest and highest mountain range in western Europe. They stretch from southeastern France, through Italy, Switzerland, Austria, and into Slovenia – a distance of about 750 miles (1,200 km). People from around the world visit the Alps to take part in sports such as skiing and mountaineering.

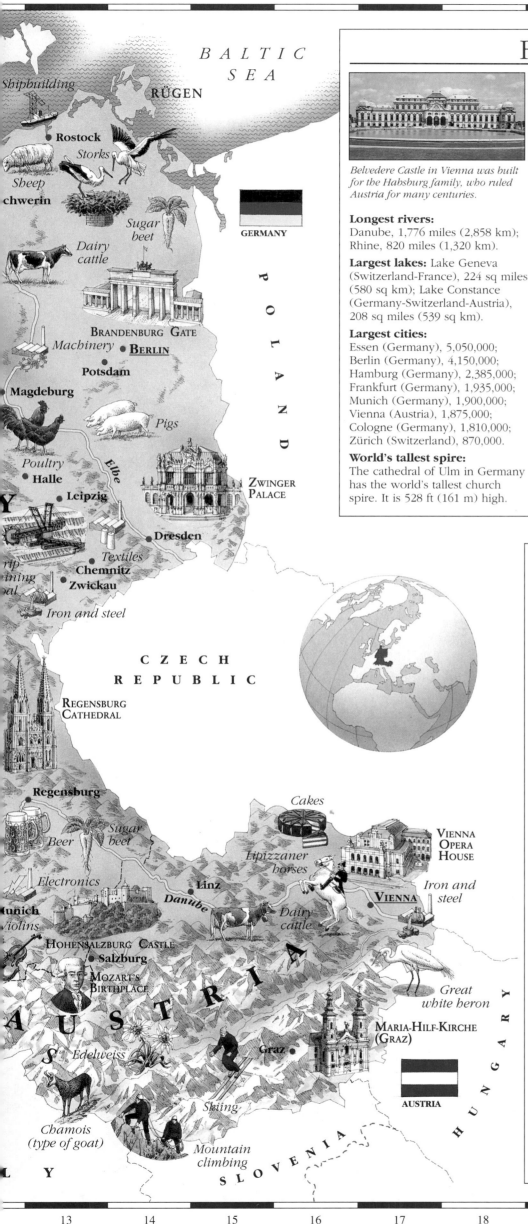

BALTIC SEA

RÜGEN

Shipbuilding

Rostock

Storks

Sheep

chwerin

Sugar beet

Dairy cattle

BRANDENBURG GATE

Machinery

BERLIN

Potsdam

Magdeburg

Pigs

Poultry

Halle

Leipzig

Elbe

ZWINGER PALACE

Dresden

Textiles

Chemnitz

Zwickau

Iron and steel

rip- ining al

P O L A N D

GERMANY

GERMANY

FACTS AND FIGURES

Belvedere Castle in Vienna was built for the Habsburg family, who ruled Austria for many centuries.

Longest rivers:
Danube, 1,776 miles (2,858 km);
Rhine, 820 miles (1,320 km).

Largest lakes: Lake Geneva (Switzerland-France), 224 sq miles (580 sq km); Lake Constance (Germany-Switzerland-Austria), 208 sq miles (539 sq km).

Largest cities:
Essen (Germany), 5,050,000;
Berlin (Germany), 4,150,000;
Hamburg (Germany), 2,385,000;
Frankfurt (Germany), 1,935,000;
Munich (Germany), 1,900,000;
Vienna (Austria), 1,875,000;
Cologne (Germany), 1,810,000;
Zürich (Switzerland), 870,000.

World's tallest spire:
The cathedral of Ulm in Germany has the world's tallest church spire. It is 528 ft (161 m) high.

Busiest canal: The Kiel Canal in Germany is the busiest in the world. In 1989 over 45,000 ships passed through it on their way between the North Sea and the Baltic Sea.

World's longest road tunnel: St. Gotthard tunnel in Switzerland runs under the Alps, and is 10.14 miles (16.32 km) long.

World's biggest roof: The glass roof over the Olympic Stadium in Munich measures 914,940 sq ft (85,000 sq m).

Many dairy cows graze on the slopes of the Alps. Their milk is used to make the famous Swiss chocolate.

AUSTRIA
Capital: Vienna
Area: 32,377 sq miles (83,855 sq km)
Population: 7,681,000
Language: German
Religion: Christian
Currency: Schilling
Government: Republic

GERMANY
Capital: Berlin
Seat of government: Bonn
Area: 137,822 sq miles (356,955 sq km)
Population: 79,710,000
Language: German
Religion: Christian
Currency: Deutsche Mark
Government: Republic

LIECHTENSTEIN
Capital: Vaduz
Area: 62 sq miles (160 sq km)
Population: 28,000
Language: German
Religion: Christian
Currency: Swiss franc
Government: Principality

SWITZERLAND
Capital: Bern
Area: 15,943 sq miles (41,293 sq km)
Population: 6,804,000
Languages: German, French, Italian
Religion: Christian
Currency: Swiss franc
Government: Republic

The city of Munich in southern Germany is famous for its annual beer festival, the Oktoberfest.

CZECH REPUBLIC

REGENSBURG CATHEDRAL

Regensburg

Beer

Sugar beet

Cakes

Lipizzaner horses

VIENNA OPERA HOUSE

Electronics

Linz

Danube

VIENNA

Iron and steel

Dairy cattle

unich iolins

HOHENSALZBURG CASTLE

Salzburg

MOZART'S BIRTHPLACE

AUSTRIA

Edelweiss

Graz

MARIA-HILF-KIRCHE (GRAZ)

Great white heron

Chamois (type of goat)

Skiing

Mountain climbing

SLOVENIA

H U N G A R Y

AUSTRIA

THE RHINE VALLEY

The Rhine is one of the longest rivers in Europe. It flows from Switzerland through Germany and the Netherlands to the North Sea. Boats can sail up the Rhine as far as Basel in Switzerland, and for this reason the river has been an important European trade route for many centuries. Products such as coal, iron ore and petroleum are still transported by barge along the Rhine today.

In western Germany, the Rhine flows through a spectacular, steep-sided valley dotted with ruined castles, some of which are 800 years old. In many places the sides of the valley have been terraced and are used for growing wine grapes.

One of the famous sights of the Rhine Valley is the Lorelei Rock, which is situated west of Wiesbaden. According to legend, a water nymph at the Lorelei sang to passing sailors and lured them to their deaths on the rocks.

ITALY

THE EASILY RECOGNIZABLE BOOT SHAPE OF ITALY is a thin, 500-mile (800-km) long peninsula in southern Europe, which stretches south into the Mediterranean Sea. Nearly three-quarters of the country is hilly or mountainous. In the north, the snow-covered Alps form a barrier between Italy and the rest of Europe. Running down the spine of the country are the Apennines, rugged mountains dotted with hill-top villages and small towns that have hardly changed for centuries. The Mediterranean islands of Sicily and Sardinia are also part of Italy.

Modern Italy, with Rome as its capital, only came into existence in 1870. Before then, the area had been a patchwork of independent city states. These states can still be seen today in Italy's 20 "regions". Two of the states have remained independent – the Vatican City in Rome and the Republic of San Marino in northeastern Italy.

Italy has been important since Roman times, when it was the center of the greatest empire Europe had ever seen. The remains of Roman roads and buildings can still be seen all over the country and beyond. In the 14th–16th centuries, Italy was the center of an important movement in the arts, called the Renaissance. Many beautiful paintings, sculptures, buildings, and poems were produced in Italy during this period. Among Italy's most famous Renaissance writers and artists were Michelangelo, Leonardo da Vinci, Raphael, and Dante. Today millions of tourists each year visit Italy's ancient cities and art treasures.

Modern Italy is an important industrial nation, with large steel, chemical, textile, and car manufacturing industries. However, many Italians still make their living from farming. The main crops are wheat, corn, rice, grapes, and olives, and there are many fishing ports around Italy's coast.

FACTS AND FIGURES

Cars, motorcycles, tractors and trucks are among Italy's most valuable exports. Major manufacturers include Fiat, Ferrari, and Lamborghini.

The city of Venice is built on about 120 islands and has canals in place of streets.

Highest mountains: Mont Blanc (Italy-France), 15,771 ft (4,807 m); Monte Rosa (Italy-Switzerland), 15,203 ft (4,634 m).

Longest river: Po, 418 miles (672 km).

Largest lakes: Lake Garda, 143 sq miles (370 sq km); Lake Maggiore, 82 sq miles (212 sq km); Lake Como, 55 sq miles (145 sq km).

Largest cities: Milan, 3,750,000; Rome, 3,175,000; Naples, 2,875,000; Turin, 1,550,000.

A horse race called the Palio takes place in Siena each year. The riders wear traditional costumes dating from the 15th century.

ITALY
Capital: Rome
Area: 116,324 sq miles (301,277 sq km)
Population: 57,830,000
Language: Italian
Religion: Christian
Currency: Lira
Government: Republic

MALTA
Capital: Valletta
Area: 122 sq miles (316 sq km)
Population: 357,000
Languages: Maltese, English
Religion: Christian
Currency: Maltese pound
Government: Republic

SAN MARINO
Capital: San Marino
Area: 24 sq miles (61 sq km)
Population: 23,000
Language: Italian
Religion: Christian
Currency: Lira
Government: Republic

VATICAN CITY
Area: 0.2 sq miles (0.4 sq km)
Population: 800

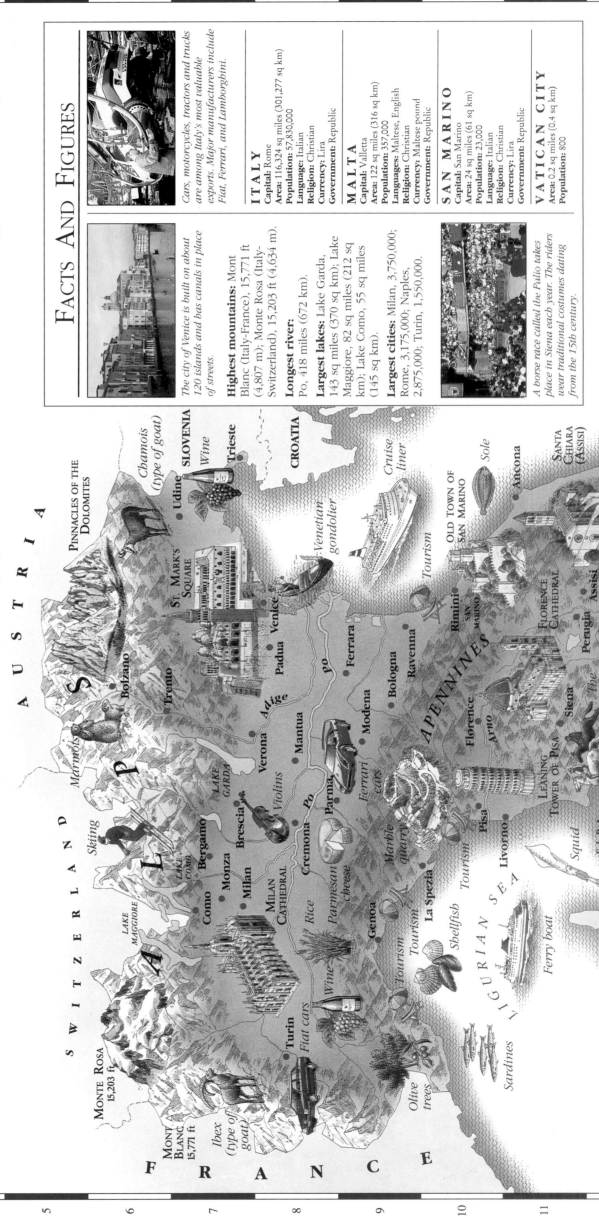

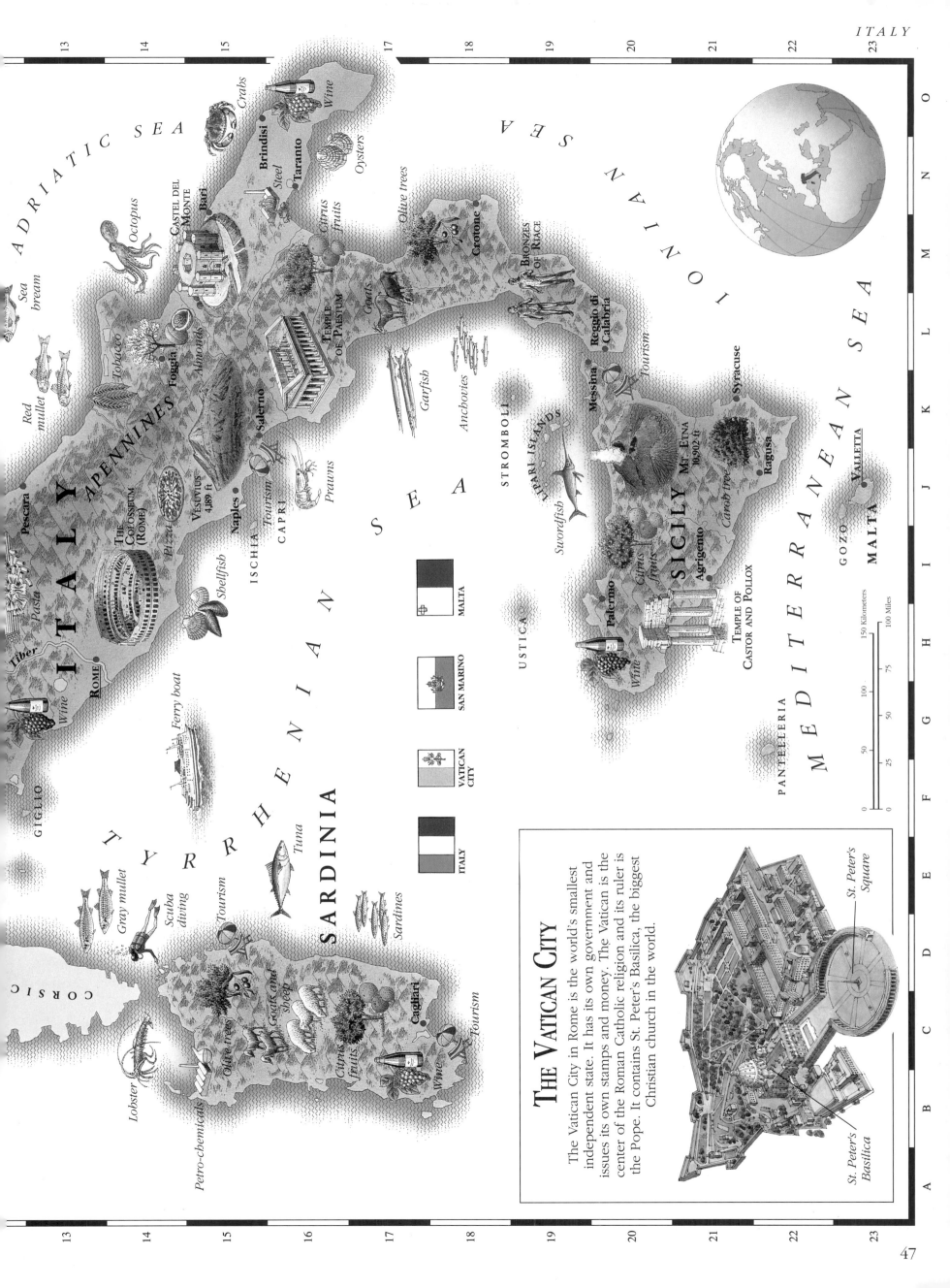

13 14 15 17 18 19 20 21 22 23

O
N
M
L
K
J
I
H
G
F
E
D
C
B
A

ADRIATIC SEA

IONIAN SEA

Crabs

Wine

Brindisi

Steel

Taranto

Oysters

Octopus

Bari

CASTEL DEL
MONTE

Citrus
fruits

Olive trees

Crotone

Sea
bream

BRONZES
OF RIACE

Red
mullet

Tobacco

Foggia

Almonds

Goats

TEMPLE
OF PAESTUM

**Reggio di
Calabria**

Tourism

Messina

Garfish

Anchovies

STROMBOLI

Syracuse

APENNINES

VESUVIUS
4,189 ft

Salerno

Tourism

CAPRI

Prawns

LIPARI ISLANDS

MT. ETNA
10,902 ft

Carob tree

Ragusa

Pescara

THE COLOSSEUM
(ROME)

Pizza

Naples

ISCHIA

Shellfish

Swordfish

SICILY

Agrigento

VALLETTA

Pasta

GOZO

MALTA

Tiber

ROME

Wine

Ferry boat

USTICA

Citrus
fruits

Palermo

TEMPLE OF
CASTOR AND POLLOX

MALTA

SAN MARINO

*VATICAN
CITY*

ITALY

Wine

PANTELLERIA

MEDITERRANEAN SEA

150 Kilometers
100 Miles
100
75
50
50
25
0

GIGLIO

TYRRHENIAN SEA

Tuna

SARDINIA

Sardines

Gray mullet

Tourism

Scuba
diving

CORSICA

Olive trees

Goats and sheep

Citrus
fruits

Cagliari

Tourism

Petro-chemicals

Lobster

Wine

THE VATICAN CITY

The Vatican City in Rome is the world's smallest independent state. It has its own government and issues its own stamps and money. The Vatican is the center of the Roman Catholic religion and its ruler is the Pope. It contains St. Peter's Basilica, the biggest Christian church in the world.

*St. Peter's
Square*

*St. Peter's
Basilica*

SPAIN AND PORTUGAL

THE COUNTRIES of Spain and Portugal occupy a large, square block of land called the Iberian Peninsula in southwestern Europe. The peninsula also contains the tiny independent state of Andorra and the British colony of Gibraltar. Over the centuries, Spain and Portugal have been invaded and settled by many different peoples, including the Romans and the Moors – an Arab people from North Africa who ruled much of Spain for nearly eight centuries.

Both Spain and Portugal have a long history of exploring and trading by sea. Christopher Columbus set out from Spain when he sailed to America in 1492. In 1497 the Portuguese explorer, Vasco da Gama, became the first person to sail around Africa to India. Settlers followed the explorers, and during the 16th century Spain and Portugal came to rule vast empires in North and South America, Asia, and Africa.

Today, many people in Spain and Portugal make their living from farming or fishing. Both countries also have important manufacturing industries, producing steel, ships, cars, chemicals, and textiles. Tourism is a major source of wealth in both countries.

PORTUGAL

THE WINE TRADE

Spain and Portugal are famous for their "fortified" wines, such as sherry and port. These contain more alcohol than normal wine because brandy is added to the grape juice to fortify, or strengthen, it. This was originally done to stop the wine going bad while it was shipped abroad. Fortified wines are left in wooden casks to mature for at least three years. Both sherry and port are named after the towns where they are produced – sherry comes from Jerez de la Frontera in southern Spain, and port from Porto in northern Portugal.

BAY OF BISCA...

Shellfish

Fish packing

Horses

Iron and steel

Gijón

Apples

Oviedo

Coal

Santand...

La Coruña

CATHEDRAL OF SANTIAGO DE COMPOSTELA

Brown bear

CAVE PAINTING (ALTAMIRA)

Santiago

Potatoes

León

Cattle

Fish packing

Vigo

Minho

COCKEREL OF BARCELOS

LEÓN CATHEDRAL

Wheat

Egyptian vulture

Textiles

Braga

Valladolid

Anchovies

Porto

Port wine

Douro

Cattle

S P

Fish packing

Mackerel

Transporting port wine

Potatoes

Salamanca

HOUSE OF SHELLS (SALAMANCA)

Segovia

Rigs

Coimbra

Ávila

Pilchards

P O R T U G A L

STATUE OF PIZARRO (TRUJILLO)

Tole...

Tagus

Olive trees

Wine

ROMAN THEATRE

TOLEDO CATHEDRAL

BELÉM TOWER

ROMAN TEMPLE (ÉVORA)

Mérida

Guadiana

Sheep

Manchego cheese

LISBON

Badajoz

Windmill

Setúbal

Bulls

CÓRDOBA MOSQUE

Fish packing

Sardines

SEVILLE CATHEDRAL

Córdoba

Guadalquivir

Cork oak

Citrus fruits

Guadiana

Pardel lynx

Seville

Holy week procession (Seville)

Tourism

Tourism

Faro

Wine

Sherry

Málaga

Lobster

Jerez de la Frontera

Cádiz

ROCK OF GIBRALTAR

GIBRALTAR

STRAIT OF GIBRALTAR

M...

Ceuta (Spain)

Tuna

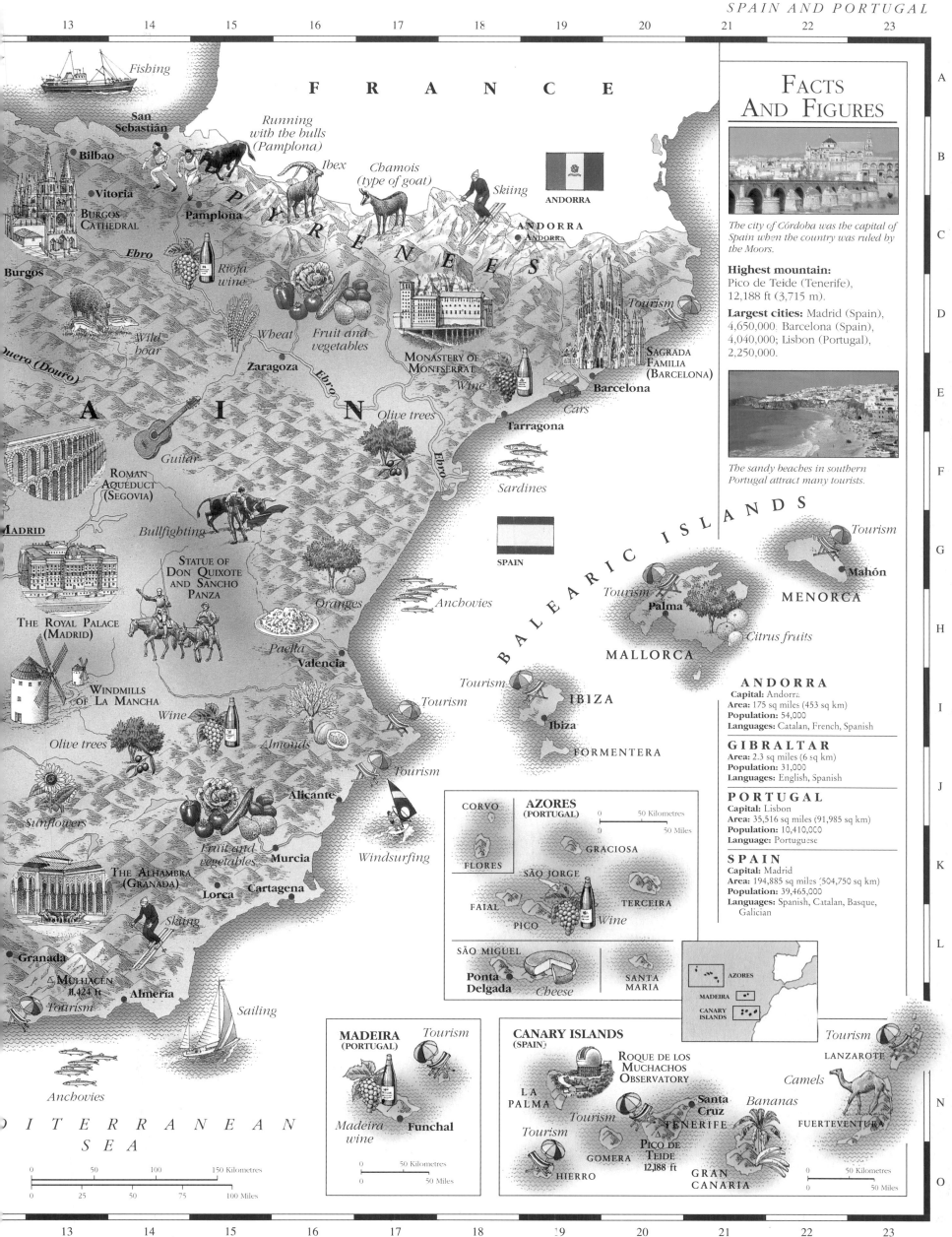

Fishing

F R A N C E

San Sebastián

Running with the bulls (Pamplona)

Ibex

Chamois (type of goat)

Skiing

ANDORRA

Bilbao

P Y R E N E E S

Vitoria

Pamplona

BURGOS CATHEDRAL

ANDORRA
Andorra

Burgos

Ebro

Rioja wine

Tourism

Wild boar

Wheat

Fruit and vegetables

MONASTERY OF MONTSERRAT

SAGRADA FAMILIA (BARCELONA)

Duero (Douro)

S P A I N

Ebro

Wine

Barcelona

ZARAGOZA

Olive trees

Cars

Tarragona

Guitar

Ebro

Sardines

ROMAN AQUÉDUCT (SEGOVIA)

SPAIN

B A L E A R I C   I S L A N D S

Tourism

MADRID

Bullfighting

STATUE OF DON QUIXOTE AND SANCHO PANZA

Oranges

Anchovies

Tourism

Mahón

Tourism

Palma

MENORCA

THE ROYAL PALACE (MADRID)

Paella

Citrus fruits

MALLORCA

Tourism

WINDMILLS OF LA MANCHA

Wine

Tourism

IBIZA

Olive trees

Almonds

Tourism

Ibiza

FORMENTERA

Sunflowers

Tourism

Alicante

MADEIRA (PORTUGAL)

Tourism

CANARY ISLANDS (SPAIN)

Tourism

LANZAROTE

Fruit and vegetables

Murcia

Windsurfing

CORVO

AZORES (PORTUGAL)

0   50 Kilometres
0   50 Miles

THE ALHAMBRA (GRANADA)

Lorca

Cartagena

GRACIOSA

FLORES

SÃO JORGE

ROQUE DE LOS MUCHACHOS OBSERVATORY

Camels

Skiing

FAIAL

TERCEIRA

LA PALMA

Bananas

Santa Cruz

FUERTEVENTURA

Granada

PICO

Wine

Tourism

TENERIFE

△ **MULHACÉN** 11,424 ft

SÃO MIGUEL

Tourism

GOMERA

PICO DE TEIDE 12,188 ft

Almería

Tourism

Ponta Delgada

Cheese

SANTA MARIA

Sailing

Madeira wine

Funchal

HIERRO

GRAN CANARIA

Anchovies

M E D I T E R R A N E A N   S E A

AZORES

MADEIRA

CANARY ISLANDS

0   50   100   150 Kilometres
0   25   50   75   100 Miles

0   50 Kilometres
0   50 Miles

0   50 Kilometres
0   50 Miles

FACTS AND FIGURES

The city of Córdoba was the capital of Spain when the country was ruled by the Moors.

Highest mountain: Pico de Teide (Tenerife), 12,188 ft (3,715 m).

Largest cities: Madrid (Spain), 4,650,000; Barcelona (Spain), 4,040,000; Lisbon (Portugal), 2,250,000.

The sandy beaches in southern Portugal attract many tourists.

ANDORRA
Capital: Andorra
Area: 175 sq miles (453 sq km)
Population: 54,000
Languages: Catalan, French, Spanish

GIBRALTAR
Area: 2.3 sq miles (6 sq km)
Population: 31,000
Languages: English, Spanish

PORTUGAL
Capital: Lisbon
Area: 35,516 sq miles (91,985 sq km)
Population: 10,410,000
Language: Portuguese

SPAIN
Capital: Madrid
Area: 194,885 sq miles (504,750 sq km)
Population: 39,465,000
Languages: Spanish, Catalan, Basque, Galician

CENTRAL AND EASTERN EUROPE

THIS REGION has always been one of the most unstable parts of Europe, and the boundaries between the countries have changed many times. After World War II, all the countries in this region, apart from Greece, became part of the "Eastern Bloc". They had communist governments and strong links with the USSR. In recent years there have been important political changes in the region. Many of the countries are now establishing democratic forms of government and are building closer links with their neighbors in Western Europe.

The northern part of this region is dominated by Poland. The country of Poland has been much fought over, and for long periods it did not exist as a separate nation. Poland is rich in coal and copper, and has large textile,

iron, steel, and shipbuilding industries. Farming is also important: the main crops are potatoes, wheat, and sugar beets. South of Poland lie the Czech Republic and Slovakia. This area was formerly one country, called Czechoslovakia. It was inhabited by two separate peoples – the Czechs and the Slovaks – who spoke different languages. In 1993 Czechoslovakia split apart to form two countries.

To the south lies the area known as the Balkans, which includes the countries of Greece, Albania, Bosnia and Herzegovina, Croatia, Macedonia, Slovenia, Yugoslavia, Bulgaria, Romania, and Hungary. The present pattern of countries in the Balkans was only formed during the rearrangement of European borders at the end of the two World Wars. More recently, the republics of Bosnia and Herzegovina, Croatia, Macedonia, and Slovenia broke away from Yugoslavia and were recognized as independent countries.

FACTS AND FIGURES

There are many picturesque old towns along the Adriatic coast of Croatia.

Largest cities:
Athens (Greece) 3,096,775;
Budapest (Hungary), 2,515,000.

Longest river:
Danube, 1,776 miles (2,858 km).

Highest mountains: Musala (Bulgaria), 9,596 ft (2,925 m); Mt Olympus (Greece), 9,570 ft (2,917 m).

Warsaw, in Poland, was badly damaged during World War II, but many old buildings have been rebuilt.

400 Kilometers
250 Miles
300
200
150
100
50
100
0
0

POLAND
HUNGARY
BULGARIA
ROMANIA
CZECH REPUBLIC
SLOVAKIA
SLOVENIA

BELARUS
UKRAINE
MOLDOVA

BALTIC SEA

Shipbuilding
Tourism
Chemicals
Gdańsk
Potatoes
Szczecin
Wooden windmills
Oder
Copper
Folk costume
Wałbrzych
Coal
Poznań
Bydgoszcz
POLAND
Vistula
Pigs
Wrocław
Wrocław
CATHEDRAL OF ST VITUS
Pilsen Lager
PRAGUE
CZECH REPUBLIC
Brno
Morava
Škoda cars
Wine
AUSTRIA
Skiing
GERMANY

Świeta Lipka Basilica
European bison
MASURIAN LAKES
Bug
PALACE OF CULTURE
WARSAW
Łódź
POZNAN TOWN HALL
Iron and steel
Coal
Lublin
Sugar beet
Wheat
Vistula
Sheep
Skiing
Katowice
Kraków
Ostrava
CARPATHIAN MTS
Kosice
SLOVAKIA
Bratislava
BRATISLAVA CASTLE
PARLIAMENT BUILDING (BUDAPEST)
Debrecen
BUDAPEST
Coal
HUNGARY
Wild boar
Chemicals
Spruce
Cattle
Machinery

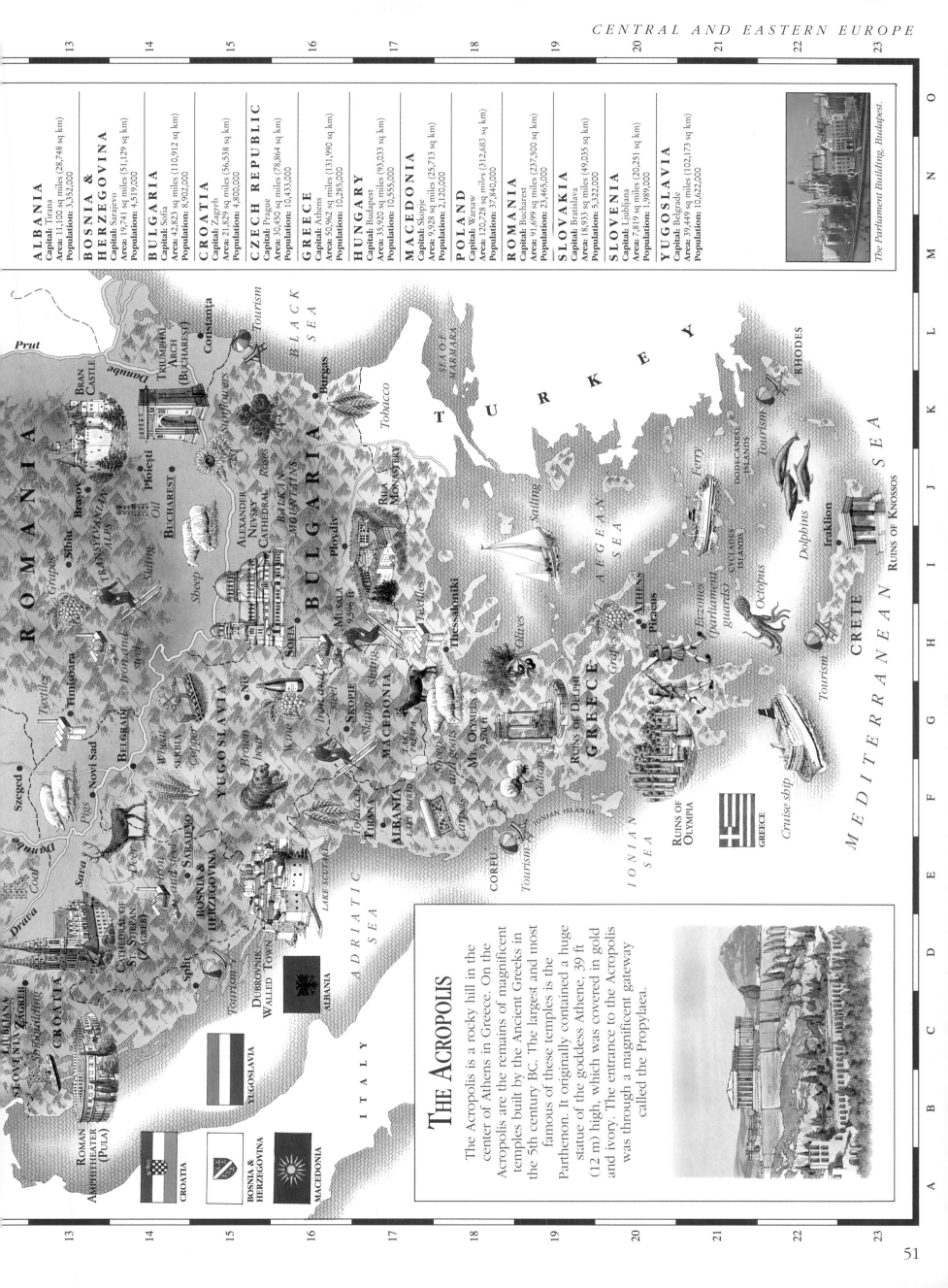

ALBANIA
Capital: Tirana
Area: 11,100 sq miles (28,748 sq km)
Population: 3,352,000

BOSNIA & HERZEGOVINA
Capital: Sarajevo
Area: 19,741 sq miles (51,129 sq km)
Population: 4,519,000

BULGARIA
Capital: Sofia
Area: 42,823 sq miles (110,912 sq km)
Population: 8,902,000

CROATIA
Capital: Zagreb
Area: 21,829 sq miles (56,538 sq km)
Population: 4,800,000

CZECH REPUBLIC
Capital: Prague
Area: 30,450 sq miles (78,864 sq km)
Population: 10,433,000

GREECE
Capital: Athens
Area: 50,962 sq miles (131,990 sq km)
Population: 10,285,000

HUNGARY
Capital: Budapest
Area: 35,920 sq miles (93,033 sq km)
Population: 10,555,000

MACEDONIA
Capital: Skopje
Area: 9,928 sq miles (25,713 sq km)
Population: 2,120,000

POLAND
Capital: Warsaw
Area: 120,728 sq miles (312,683 sq km)
Population: 37,840,000

ROMANIA
Capital: Bucharest
Area: 91,699 sq miles (237,500 sq km)
Population: 23,465,000

SLOVAKIA
Capital: Bratislava
Area: 18,933 sq miles (49,035 sq km)
Population: 5,322,000

SLOVENIA
Capital: Ljubljana
Area: 7,819 sq miles (20,251 sq km)
Population: 1,989,000

YUGOSLAVIA
Capital: Belgrade
Area: 39,449 sq miles (102,173 sq km)
Population: 10,622,000

The Parliament Building, Budapest.

THE ACROPOLIS

The Acropolis is a rocky hill in the center of Athens in Greece. On the Acropolis are the remains of magnificent temples built by the Ancient Greeks in the 5th century BC. The largest and most famous of these temples is the Parthenon. It originally contained a huge statue of the goddess Athene, 39 ft (12 m) high, which was covered in gold and ivory. The entrance to the Acropolis was through a magnificent gateway called the Propylaea.

ASIA

ASIA is the largest continent in the world, occupying nearly a third of the world's total land area. It contains the world's highest point (Mount Everest), as well as its lowest (the Dead Sea). Asia also has the largest population of any continent – six out of every ten people in the world live there. All the world's major religions – including Judaism, Islam, Buddhism, Christianity, Confucianism, and Hinduism – originated in Asia.

In a continent of this size, stretching from the Arctic to the equator, there are great contrasts. The climate ranges from some of the coldest places on earth to some of the hottest, and from some of the driest places to some of the wettest. Asia contains the world's largest country (Russia) and some of its smallest countries. In parts of Asia there are huge concentrations of people, yet there are also vast regions which are almost uninhabited.

Siberia, the Asian part of Russia, is mainly covered by coniferous forest. It is bitterly cold in winter, and few people live there. Bordering Russia in the east is China. Most of China's one billion people live in the eastern part of the country where the land is good for farming.

Guilin, China.

Bronze Buddah, Kamakura, Japan.

The population of the Gobi desert and the high Plateau of Tibet is very small. South of the Himalayas, the world's highest mountain range, lies Southern Asia, which is often called the Indian subcontinent. Around one billion people live there, mainly along the fertile coasts and on the plains of the Ganges and Indus rivers in the north.

Southwestern Asia is also known as the Middle East. The world's earliest known civilizations grew up here in the area called the Fertile Crescent, which extends from the Mediterranean Sea across Syria to the land between the Tigris and Euphrates rivers. Among the ancient peoples of the Fertile Crescent were the Sumerians, Assyrians, Babylonians, and Hebrews. This area contrasts sharply with the almost empty deserts of the Arabian Peninsula, occupied by the oil-rich nations of the Persian Gulf, such as Saudi Arabia, Qatar, and Bahrain.

Southeastern Asia is situated along the equator. Much of the region is made up of thousands of islands, large and small. These include the countries of Indonesia, Malaysia, and the Philippines.

The Palace of the Winds, Jaipur, India.

FACTS ABOUT ASIA

Area: 16,838,365 sq miles (43,608,000 sq km).

Population: 3,074,000,000.

Number of independent countries: 47 (this includes 97 percent of Turkey, and 77 percent of Russia).

Largest countries: The Asian part of Russia, 5,065,499 sq miles (13,119,582 sq km) – this is 77 percent of the total area of Russia; China, 3,689,631 sq miles (9,556,100 sq km).

Most populated countries: China, 1,181,580,000 (the largest population in the world); India, 874,150,000.

Largest cities: Tokyo (Japan), 30,300,000; Seoul (South Korea), 15,850,000; Shanghai (China), 9,300,000.

Highest mountains: Mt. Everest (Nepal-China), the highest in the world, 29,028 ft (8,848 m); K2 (Qogir Feng) (Pakistan-China), 28,250 ft (8,611 m).

Longest rivers: Yangtze (Chang Jiang), 3,915 miles (6,300 km); Yellow River (Huang He), 3,395 miles (5,463 km); Ob-Irtysh, 3,362 miles (5,410 km); Amur, 2,761 miles (4,443 km).

Main deserts: Gobi (Mongolia-China), about 500,000 sq miles (1,295,000 sq km); Thar (Pakistan-India), about 74,000 sq miles (192,000 sq km).

Largest lakes: Caspian Sea, the largest in the world, 143,205 sq miles (371,000 sq km); Aral Sea (Kazakhstan-Uzbekistan), 14,865 sq miles (38,500 sq km).

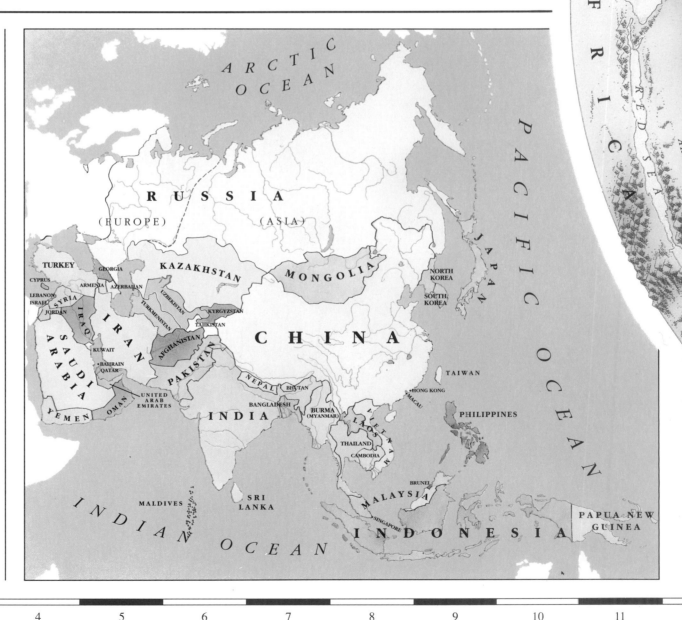

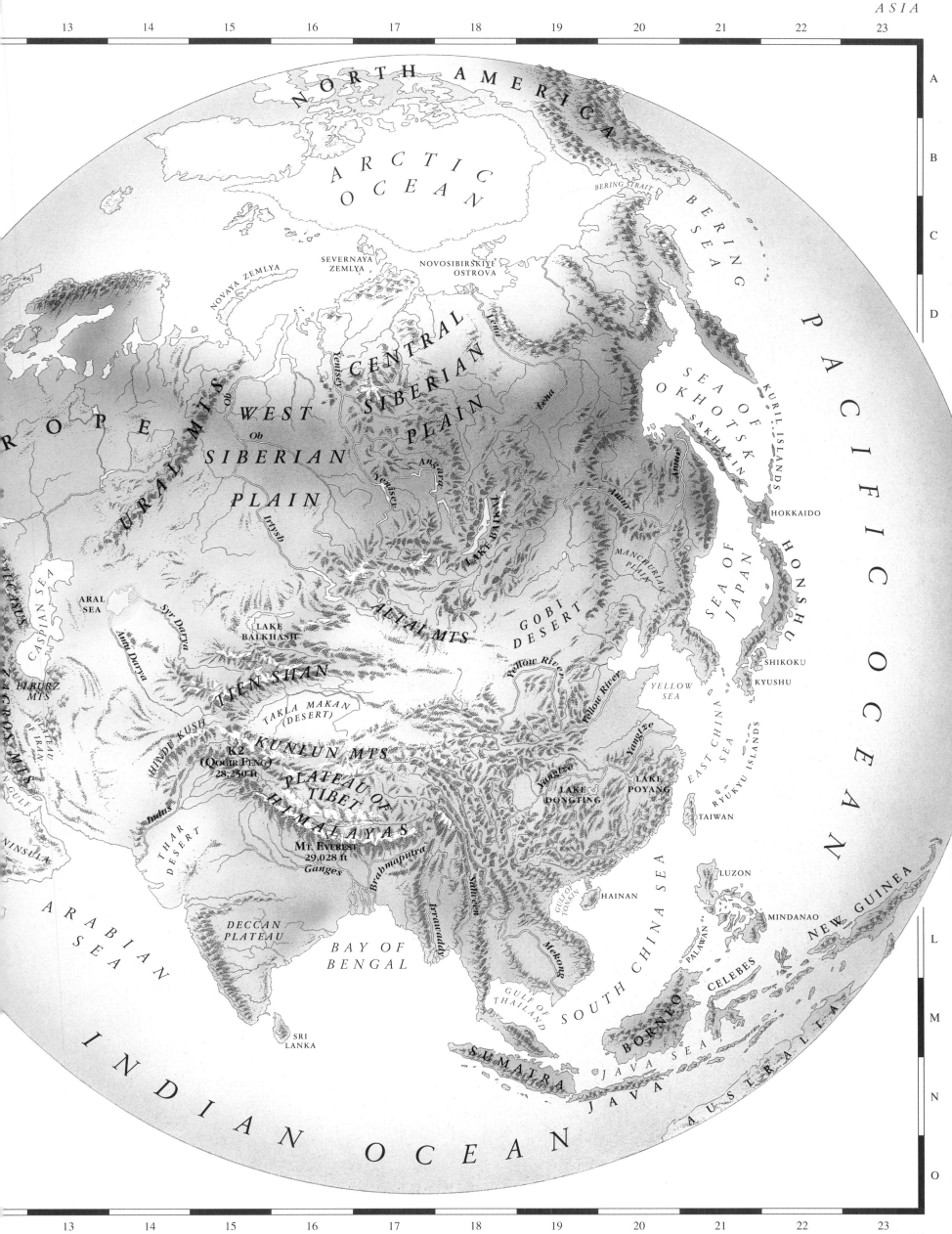

NORTH AMERICA

ARCTIC
OCEAN

BERING STRAIT

BERING
SEA

NOVAYA ZEMLYA
SEVERNAYA
ZEMLYA
NOVOSIBIRSKIYE
OSTROVA

Yenisei

Lena

CENTRAL
SIBERIAN
PLAIN

Ob

WEST
Ob

SIBERIAN
PLAIN

URAL MTS

Irtysh

Yenisei

Angara

LAKE BAIKAL

Amur

SEA OF
OKHOTSK

KURIL ISLANDS

SAKHALIN

HOKKAIDO

EUROPE

CASPIAN SEA

ARAL
SEA

Syr Darya

Amu Darya

LAKE
BALKHASH

ALTAI MTS

GOBI
DESERT

MANCHURIAN
PLAIN

SEA OF
JAPAN

HONSHU

CAUCASUS

ELBURZ
MTS

ZAGROS MTS

PLATEAU
OF IRAN

GULF

HINDU KUSH

TIEN SHAN

TAKLA MAKAN
(DESERT)

K2
(QOGIR FENG)
28,250 ft

KUNLUN MTS

PLATEAU OF
TIBET

HIMALAYAS

Yellow River

Yellow River

YELLOW
SEA

Yangtze

LAKE
DONGTING

LAKE
POYANG

Yangtze

EAST CHINA
SEA

SHIKOKU

KYUSHU

RYUKYU ISLANDS

TAIWAN

PENINSULA

Indus

THAR
DESERT

DECCAN
PLATEAU

Mt. Everest
29,028 ft
Ganges

Brahmaputra

Salween

BAY OF
BENGAL

SRI
LANKA

Irrawaddy

Mekong

GULF OF
THAILAND

GULF OF
TONN

HAINAN

SOUTH CHINA SEA

LUZON

MINDANAO

PALAWAN

NEW GUINEA

CELEBES

BORNEO

ARABIAN
SEA

SUMATRA

JAVA SEA

JAVA

AUSTRALIA

INDIAN OCEAN

PACIFIC OCEAN

NORTHERN EURASIA

THIS REGION SPANS TWO CONTINENTS, Europe in the west and Asia in the east. They are separated by the Ural Mountains. The Asian part is much bigger, occupying about 75 percent of the land area, but only about 35 percent of the people live there. To the east lies Siberia, much of which is covered by a huge uninhabited wilderness of coniferous trees. The climate there is extremely cold, and in winter the temperature in the north regularly falls below -45°C (-49°F), but this area is rich in precious stones and oil.

From 1922 to 1991, northern Eurasia was one vast country, called the Union of Soviet Socialist Republics, or Soviet Union. It was the world's largest country and was made up of 15 republics, all with communist governments. In 1991, the Soviet Union split apart and all the republics became independent countries. The largest of them – Russia – remained dominant and succeeded in drawing many of the new nations together in a Commonwealth of Independent States.

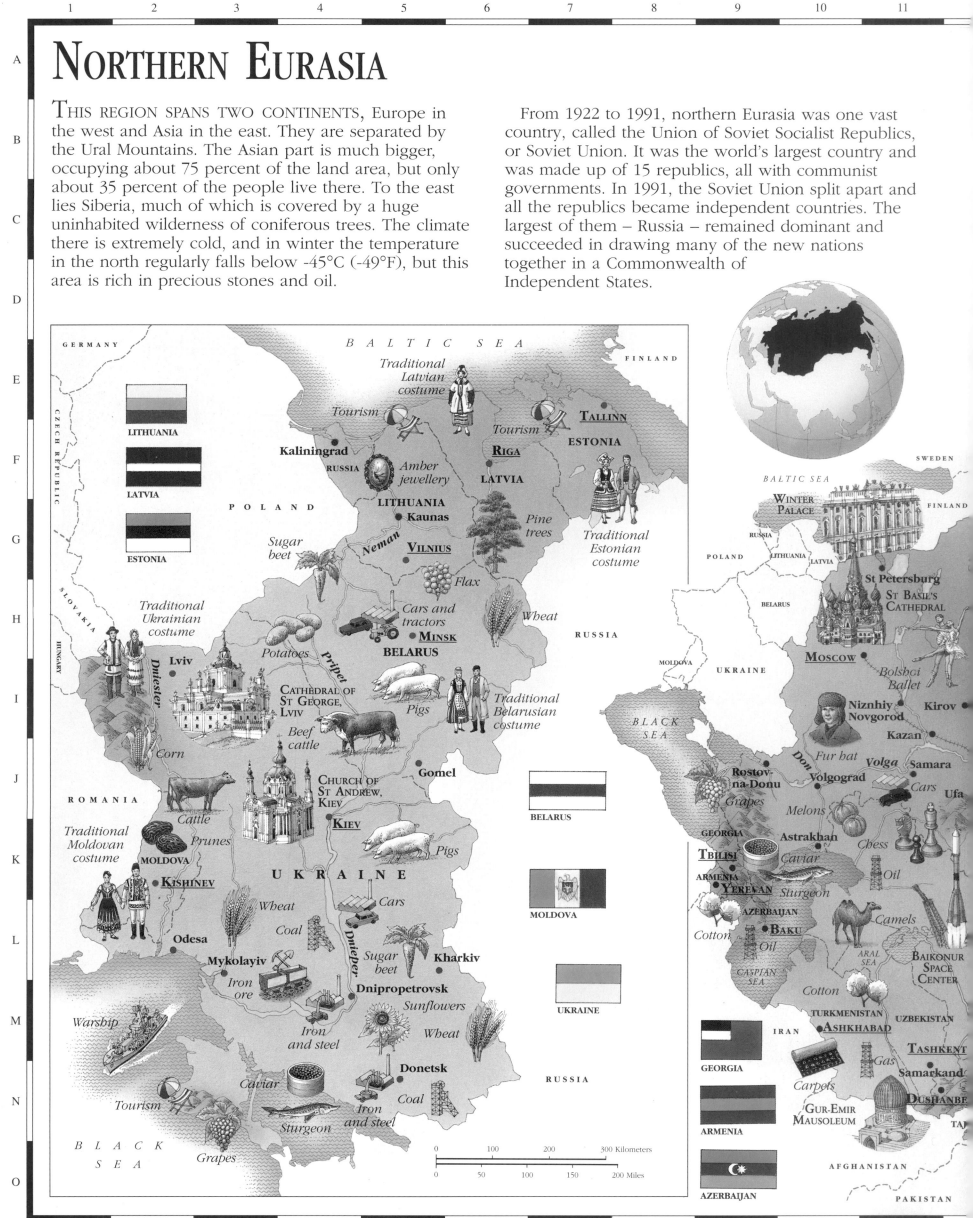

FACTS AND FIGURES

The Cathedral of the Annunciation, the Kremlin, Moscow.

Largest lake: Caspian Sea (the largest lake in the world) covers an area of 143,205 sq miles (371,000 sq km).

World's longest railway: Trans-Siberian, Moscow to Nakhodka near Vladivostok, 5,864 miles (9,438 km).

ARMENIA
Capital: Yerevan
Area: 11,506 sq miles (29,800 sq km)
Population: 3,360,000
Languages: Armenian, Russian

AZERBAIJAN
Capital: Baku
Area: 33,436 sq miles (86,600 sq km)
Population: 7,170,000
Language: Azeri, Russian

BELARUS
Capital: Minsk
Area: 80,155 sq miles (207,600 sq km)
Population: 10,390,000
Languages: Byelorussian, Russian

ESTONIA
Capital: Tallinn
Area: 17,413 sq miles (45,100 sq km)
Population: 1,606,000
Language: Estonian, Russian

GEORGIA
Capital: Tbilisi
Area: 26,911 sq miles (69,700 sq km)
Population: 5,550,000
Language: Georgian, Russian

KAZAKHSTAN
Capital: Alma-Ata
Area: 1,049,156 sq miles (2,717,300 sq km)
Population: 16,880,000
Languages: Qazaq, Russian

KYRGYZSTAN
Capital: Bishkek
Area: 76,641 sq miles (198,500 sq km)
Population: 4,385,000
Languages: Kirghiz

LATVIA
Capital: Riga
Area: 24,595 sq miles (63,700 sq km)
Population: 2,737,000
Languages: Latvian, Russian

LITHUANIA
Capital: Vilnius
Area: 25,174 sq miles (65,200 sq km)
Population: 3,767,000
Language: Lithuanian, Polish, Russian

MOLDOVA
Capital: Kishinev
Area: 13,012 sq miles (33,700 sq km)
Population: 4,440,000
Language: Romanian

RUSSIA
Capital: Moscow
Area: 6,592,849 sq miles (17,075,400 sq km)
Population: 150,505,000
Language: Russian

TAJIKISTAN
Capital: Dushanbe
Area: 55,251 sq miles (143,100 sq km)
Population: 5,210,000
Languages: Tajik

TURKMENISTAN
Capital: Ashkhabad
Area: 188,456 sq miles (488,100 sq km)
Population: 3,615,000
Languages: Turkmen, Russian

UKRAINE
Capital: Kiev
Area: 233,090 sq miles (603,700 sq km)
Population: 52,800,000
Languages: Ukrainian, Russian

UZBEKISTAN
Capital: Tashkent
Area: 172,742 sq miles (447,400 sq km)
Population: 20,325,000
Languages: Uzbek, Russian

SOUTHWESTERN ASIA

SOUTHWEST ASIA, also known as the Middle East, lies at the juncture of three continents – Asia, Africa, and Europe. It contains many varied landscapes and cultures. The countries surrounding the Mediterranean are wetter than the others, and crops such as citrus fruits, olives, and wheat are grown here. To the south stretch the huge deserts of Saudi Arabia. Earlier this century, the world's largest deposits of oil were discovered in the countries around the Persian Gulf. The oilfields in the region now supply the world.

Some of the world's first settled farming communities and towns grew up in the rich farmlands of the Fertile Crescent, which stretches from the Mediterranean to the area between the Tigris and Euphrates rivers. In recent years, Southwest Asia has been an unsettled region, troubled by a revolution in Iran and a long and bitter war between Iran and Iraq. Civil war in Lebanon has claimed many lives, and there have also been wars between Israel and its Arab neighbors.

JERUSALEM

Dome of the Rock

Wailing Wall

Jerusalem is a holy place for Christians, Moslems, and Jews, and it is visited by millions of people each year. The Church of the Holy Sepulcher is built where Christians believe Christ was buried. The gold-topped Dome of the Rock is a mosque built where Moslems believe Mohammed ascended into heaven. The Wailing Wall, where Jews go to pray, is all that remains of the Jewish Temple built by King Herod in the 1st century BC.

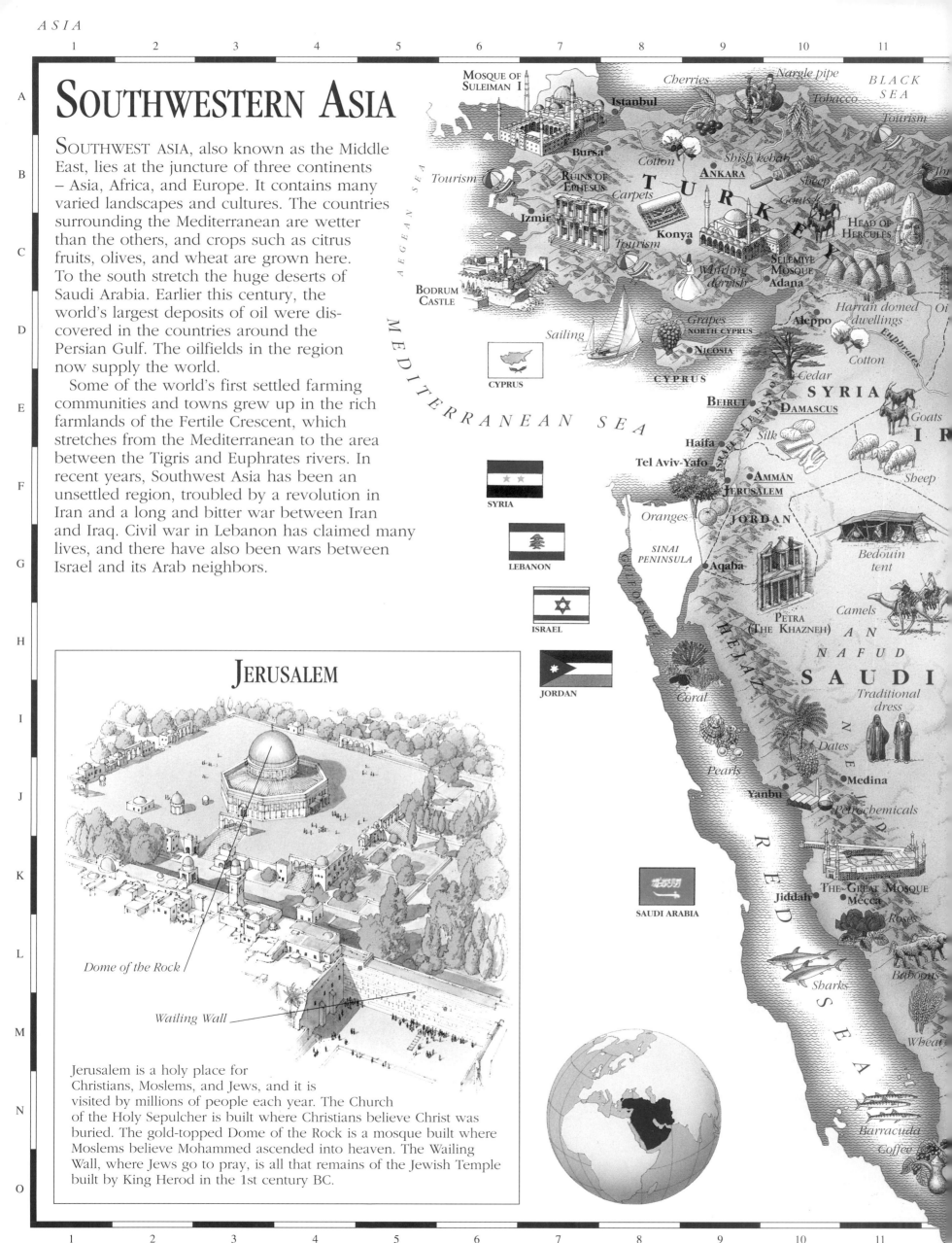

CYPRUS

SYRIA

LEBANON

ISRAEL

JORDAN

SAUDI ARABIA

Mosque of Suleiman I

Istanbul

Bursa

Ruins of Ephesus

Izmir

Bodrum Castle

Tourism

Sailing

Cotton

Carpets

Tourism

Grapes
NORTH CYPRUS

Nicosia

CYPRUS

ANKARA

Konya

Whirling dervish

SELEMIYE MOSQUE

Adana

Cherries

Nargile pipe

Tobacco

Shish kebab

Sheep

Goats

BLACK SEA

Tourism

HEAD OF HERCULES

Harran domed dwellings

Aleppo

Cotton

Cedar

SYRIA

BEIRUT

DAMASCUS

Silk

Haifa

Tel Aviv-Yafo

AMMÁN

JERUSALEM

Oranges

JORDAN

SINAI PENINSULA

Aqaba

Euphrates

Goats

Sheep

Bedouin tent

Camels

Petra (The Khazneh)

A N
N A F U D

S A U D I

HEJAZ

Coral

Pearls

Dates

Traditional dress

Medina

Yanbu

Petrochemicals

THE GREAT MOSQUE

Jiddah

Mecca

Roses

RED SEA

Sharks

Baboons

Wheat

Barracuda

Coffee

GEORGIA

Tea

ARMENIA

Bears

Tobacco

AZERBAIJAN

CASPIAN SEA

TURKMENISTAN

MT. ARARAT 16,804 ft

LAKE VAN

Oil

Apples

Melons

Kurdish dress

Tabriz

Tea

Sturgeon

Mashhad

Rice

Silk

Caviar

Mosul

Oil

Carpets

TEHRAN

LAKE NAMAK

Turquoise

HAYDAR KHANAH MOSQUE

Bakhtaran

Qom

THE ROYAL MOSQUE

Traditional dress

BAGHDAD

IRAQ

Tigris

Dates

Esfahan

Pigeon towers

Cotton

ZIGGURAT AT UR

Oil

I R A N

Textiles

Chemicals

Oil

Ahvaz

PERSEPOLIS (PALACE STAIRCASE)

Goats

Arab marsh reed house

Basra

Abadan

Shiraz

Oil

Oil

Sheep

KUWAIT

Gas

BAM

KUWAIT

Gas

A R A B I A

Cattle

Oil

Petrochemicals

PERSIAN GULF

Oil

Oil

Gas

STRAIT OF HORMUZ

Sardines

GULF OF OMAN

Yashmak (face veil)

Oil

Al Jubayl

Oil

Dhow (Arab boat)

A D D A H N A

Oil

Oil

DOHA

Oil tanker

Oil

Dubai

OMAN

RIYADH

QATAR

ABU DHABI

MUSCAT

Arab horses

Falconry

UNITED ARAB EMIRATES

Dates

Dhow (Arab boat)

A R A B I A N D E S E R T

Khanjar (Arab dagger)

Oil

Oil

Incense burner

Sand dunes 700 ft

Kummas Omani (embroidered cap)

Oil

JIZAN DAM

R U B A L K H A L I

O M A N

THIS BORDER HAS NEVER BEEN FORMALLY DEFINED

Arabian oryx

Ancient painted house

Camels

Frankincense (Boswellia tree)

Oil tanker

A R A B I A N S E A

Y E M E N

Dates

Dhow (Arab boat)

SANA

Cotton

Aden

FACTS AND FIGURES

Dhow (Arab boat) off the Yemen coast.

Largest city: Tehran (Iran), 7,500,000.

Hottest capital: Riyadh, in Saudi Arabia, is the hottest capital city in the world, with average July temperatures of over 104°F (40°C).

Sand dunes in the Rub al Khali (The Empty Quarter) in Saudi Arabia. Dunes are formed by the wind, which blows the sand into mounds.

BAHRAIN
Capital: Al Manāmah
Area: 267 sq miles (691 sq km)

CYPRUS
Capital: Nicosia
Area: 3,571 sq miles (9,251 sq km)

IRAN
Capital: Tehran
Area: 636,457 sq miles (1,638,057 sq km)

IRAQ
Capital: Baghdād
Area: 169,235 sq miles (438,317 sq km)

ISRAEL
Capital: Jerusalem
Area: 8,017 sq miles (20,770 sq km)
Plus the occupied territories of Gaza Strip, Golan Heights, and West Bank, total area 2,947 sq miles (7,632 sq km)

JORDAN
Capital: Ammān
Area: 35,135 sq miles (91,000 sq km)

KUWAIT
Capital: Kuwait
Area: 6,880 sq miles (17,818 sq km)

LEBANON
Capital: Beirut
Area: 4,015 sq miles (10,400 sq km)

OMAN
Capital: Muscat
Area: 82,030 sq miles (212,457 sq km)

QATAR
Capital: Doha
Area: 4,416 sq miles (11,437 sq km)

SAUDI ARABIA
Capital: Riyadh
Area: 830,000 sq miles (2,149,690 sq km)

SYRIA
Capital: Damascus
Area: 71,498 sq miles (185,180 sq km)

TURKEY
Capital: Ankara
Area: 300,948 sq miles (779.452 sq km)

UNITED ARAB EMIRATES
Capital: Abu Dhabi
Area: 32,278 sq miles (83,600 sq km)

YEMEN
Capital: Sana
Area: 205,356 sq miles (531,869 sq km)

TURKEY

IRAQ

IRAN

OMAN

KUWAIT

BAHRAIN

YEMEN

QATAR

UNITED ARAB EMIRATES

SOUTHERN ASIA

THE LARGEST COUNTRY in Southern Asia is India, and the region is often called the "Indian subcontinent". Over one billion people live in Southern Asia – around 22 percent of the world's total population.

Most people in Southern Asia live in the wetter areas on the coasts and on the fertile plains of the Indus and Ganges rivers. Nearly three-quarters of the people earn their living from farming. Water is vital, and farmers depend on the monsoon rains, which fall between May and November. The most important crop is rice.

India was united in the 16th and 17th centuries under the Mogul emperors. Then, in the 18th century, the country became part of the British Empire. India gained independence from Britain in 1947, when it was divided into two countries with different religions: Moslem Pakistan and Hindu India. In 1971 the eastern part of Pakistan became a separate country, called Bangladesh.

Today Pakistan and India are the most industrial countries in Southern Asia. Pakistan has textile, food processing, and chemical industries. India produces oil, coal, iron ore, manganese, and copper, and has a variety of industries, including iron and steel, car manufacturing, and computers.

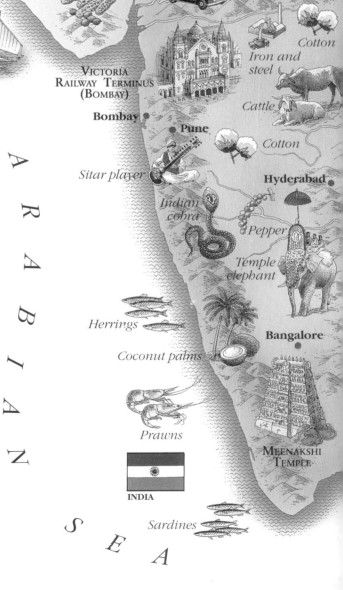

THE TAJ MAHAL

The Taj Mahal was built near Agra in northern India by the Mogul Emperor Shah Jehan as a burial place for his wife, the Empress Mumtaz Mahal. It was built between 1630 and 1650 and about 20,000 laborers worked on the building. The Taj Mahal is made of white marble, which was brought 310 miles (500 km) from Rajasthan. The interior is decorated with precious and semiprecious stones.

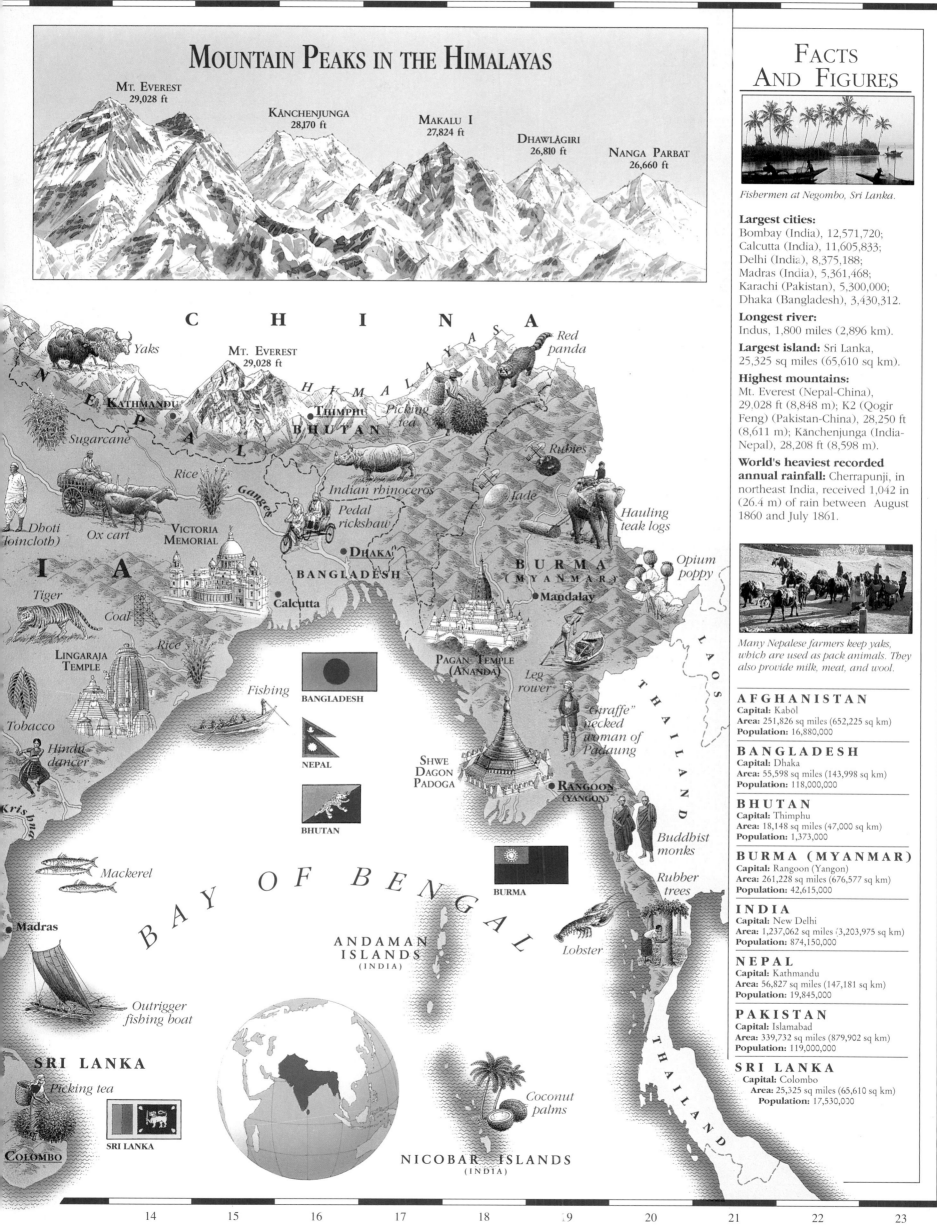

MOUNTAIN PEAKS IN THE HIMALAYAS

MT. EVEREST
29,028 ft

KĀNCHENJUNGA
28,170 ft

MAKALU I
27,824 ft

DHAWLĀGIRI
26,810 ft

NANGA PARBAT
26,660 ft

Map labels

Yaks

Red panda

C H I N A

MT. EVEREST
29,028 ft

H I M A L A Y A S

Picking tea

N E P A L

KATHMANDU

THIMPHU

BHUTAN

Sugarcane

Rice

Ganges

Indian rhinoceros

Rubies

Pedal rickshaw

Jade

Hauling teak logs

Dhoti (loincloth)

Ox cart

VICTORIA MEMORIAL

DHAKA

BANGLADESH

Opium poppy

B U R M A (MYANMAR)

Mandalay

Tiger

Calcutta

Coal

Rice

I N D I A

Lingaraja Temple

PAGAN TEMPLE (ANANDA)

Leg rower

Tobacco

Hindu dancer

Fishing

BANGLADESH

NEPAL

BHUTAN

"Giraffe" necked woman of Padaung

T H A I L A N D

L A O S

SHWE DAGON PADOGA

RANGOON (YANGON)

Buddhist monks

BURMA

Rubber trees

Krishna

Mackerel

B A Y   O F   B E N G A L

ANDAMAN ISLANDS (INDIA)

Lobster

Madras

Outrigger fishing boat

SRI LANKA

Picking tea

SRI LANKA

COLOMBO

Coconut palms

NICOBAR ISLANDS (INDIA)

THAILAND

FACTS AND FIGURES

Fishermen at Negombo, Sri Lanka.

Largest cities:
Bombay (India), 12,571,720;
Calcutta (India), 11,605,833;
Delhi (India), 8,375,188;
Madras (India), 5,361,468;
Karachi (Pakistan), 5,300,000;
Dhaka (Bangladesh), 3,430,312.

Longest river:
Indus, 1,800 miles (2,896 km).

Largest island: Sri Lanka,
25,325 sq miles (65,610 sq km).

Highest mountains:
Mt. Everest (Nepal-China),
29,028 ft (8,848 m); K2 (Qogir
Feng) (Pakistan-China), 28,250 ft
(8,611 m); Kānchenjunga (India-
Nepal), 28,208 ft (8,598 m).

**World's heaviest recorded
annual rainfall:** Cherrapunji, in
northeast India, received 1,042 in
(26.4 m) of rain between August
1860 and July 1861.

Many Nepalese farmers keep yaks,
which are used as pack animals. They
also provide milk, meat, and wool.

AFGHANISTAN
Capital: Kabōl
Area: 251,826 sq miles (652,225 sq km)
Population: 16,880,000

BANGLADESH
Capital: Dhaka
Area: 55,598 sq miles (143,998 sq km)
Population: 118,000,000

BHUTAN
Capital: Thimphu
Area: 18,148 sq miles (47,000 sq km)
Population: 1,373,000

BURMA (MYANMAR)
Capital: Rangoon (Yangon)
Area: 261,228 sq miles (676,577 sq km)
Population: 42,615,000

INDIA
Capital: New Delhi
Area: 1,237,062 sq miles (3,203,975 sq km)
Population: 874,150,000

NEPAL
Capital: Kathmandu
Area: 56,827 sq miles (147,181 sq km)
Population: 19,845,000

PAKISTAN
Capital: Islamabad
Area: 339,732 sq miles (879,902 sq km)
Population: 119,000,000

SRI LANKA
Capital: Colombo
Area: 25,325 sq miles (65,610 sq km)
Population: 17,530,000

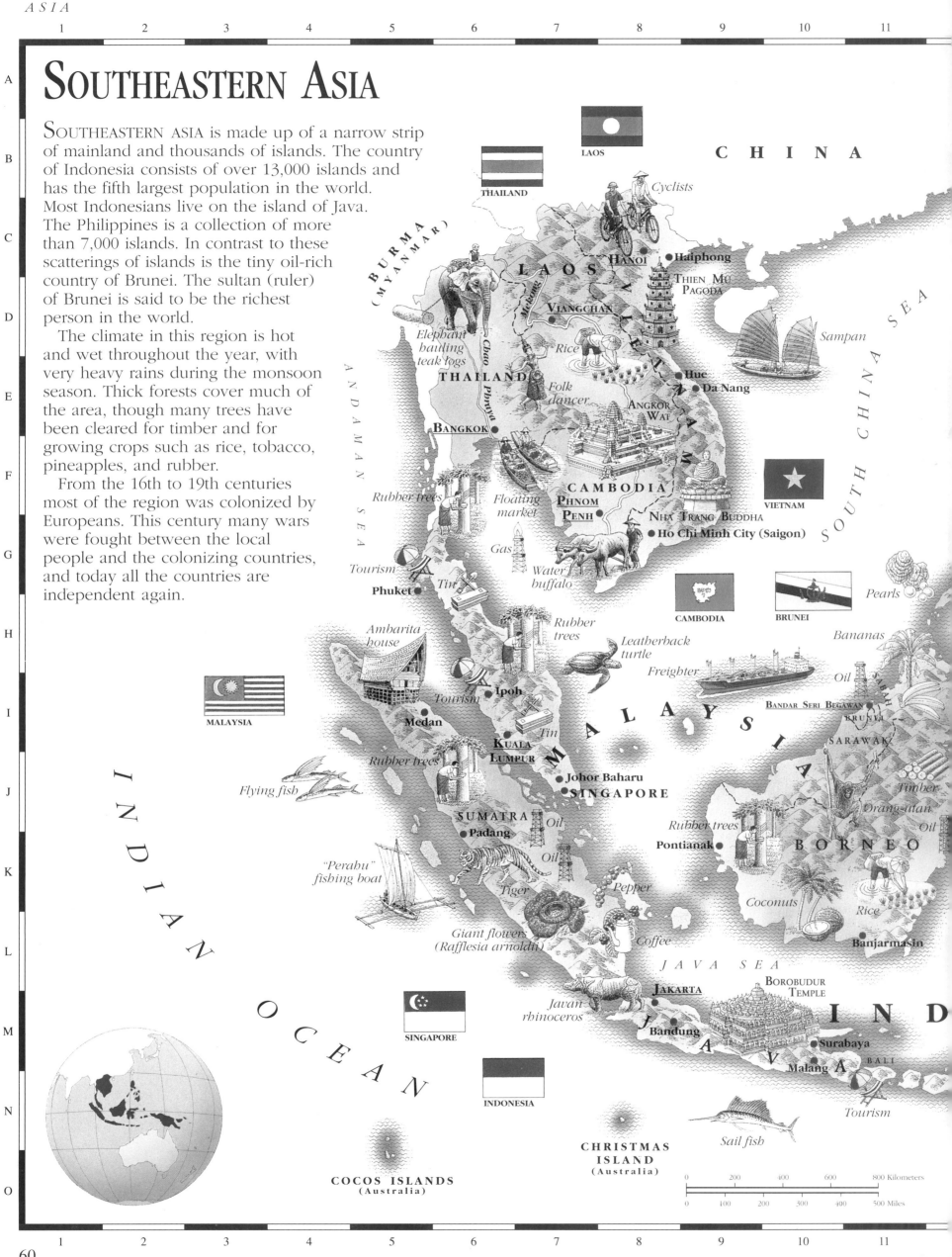

SOUTHEASTERN ASIA

SOUTHEASTERN ASIA is made up of a narrow strip of mainland and thousands of islands. The country of Indonesia consists of over 13,000 islands and has the fifth largest population in the world. Most Indonesians live on the island of Java. The Philippines is a collection of more than 7,000 islands. In contrast to these scatterings of islands is the tiny oil-rich country of Brunei. The sultan (ruler) of Brunei is said to be the richest person in the world.

The climate in this region is hot and wet throughout the year, with very heavy rains during the monsoon season. Thick forests cover much of the area, though many trees have been cleared for timber and for growing crops such as rice, tobacco, pineapples, and rubber.

From the 16th to 19th centuries most of the region was colonized by Europeans. This century many wars were fought between the local people and the colonizing countries, and today all the countries are independent again.

LAOS

THAILAND

CHINA

Cyclists

LAOS

HANOI · Haiphong

VIANGCHAN

Thien Mu Pagoda

Mekong

Elephant hauling teak logs

Chao Phraya

THAILAND

Rice

Folk dancer

Hue · Da Nang

BANGKOK

ANGKOR WAT

Sampan

Rubber trees

Floating market

CAMBODIA

PHNOM PENH

Nha Trang Buddha

Ho Chi Minh City (Saigon)

VIETNAM

Gas

Water buffalo

Tourism

PHUKET

Tin

Rubber trees

Leatherback turtle

CAMBODIA

BRUNEI

Pearls

Bananas

Freighter

Oil

Ambarita house

Tourism

Ipoh

MALAYSIA

MEDAN

KUALA LUMPUR

Tin

Bandar Seri Begawan

BRUNEI

SARAWAK

MALAYSIA

Rubber trees

Johor Baharu

SINGAPORE

Timber

Orang-utan

Oil

INDIAN OCEAN

Flying fish

"Perahu" fishing boat

SUMATRA

PADANG

Oil

Oil

Rubber trees

PONTIANAK

BORNEO

Coconuts

Rice

Tiger

Pepper

Coffee

Banjarmasin

Giant flowers (Rafflesia arnoldii)

JAVA SEA

SINGAPORE

INDONESIA

Javan rhinoceros

JAKARTA

BOROBUDUR TEMPLE

BANDUNG

JAVA

Surabaya

Malang

BALI

Tourism

Sail fish

COCOS ISLANDS (Australia)

CHRISTMAS ISLAND (Australia)

| 0 | 200 | 400 | 600 | 800 Kilometers |
| 0 | 100 | 200 | 300 | 400 | 500 Miles |

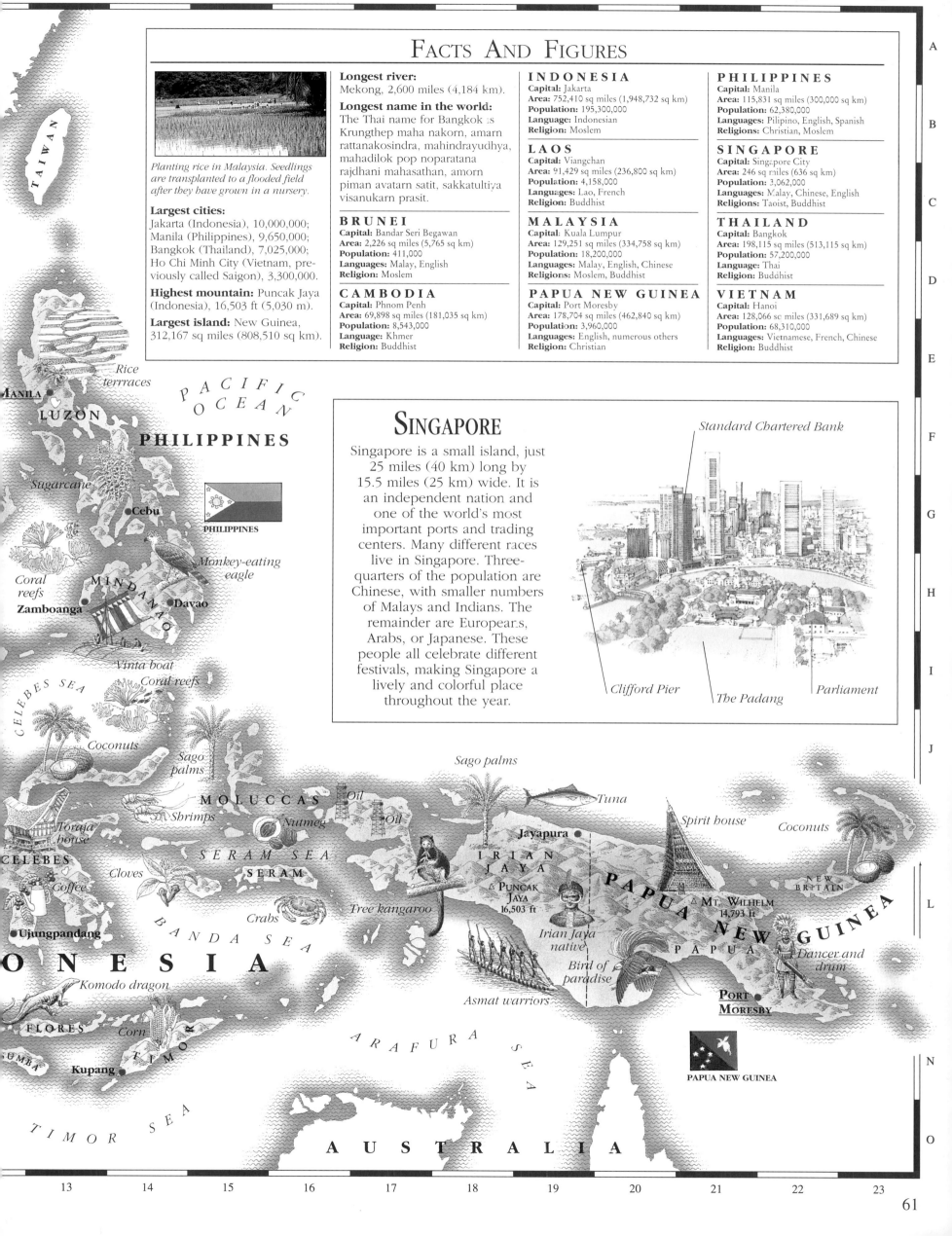

FACTS AND FIGURES

Planting rice in Malaysia. Seedlings are transplanted to a flooded field after they have grown in a nursery.

Largest cities:
Jakarta (Indonesia), 10,000,000;
Manila (Philippines), 9,650,000;
Bangkok (Thailand), 7,025,000;
Ho Chi Minh City (Vietnam, previously called Saigon), 3,300,000.

Highest mountain: Puncak Jaya (Indonesia), 16,503 ft (5,030 m).

Largest island: New Guinea, 312,167 sq miles (808,510 sq km).

Longest river:
Mekong, 2,600 miles (4,184 km).

Longest name in the world:
The Thai name for Bangkok is Krungthep maha nakorn, amarn rattanakosindra, mahindrayudhya, mahadilok pop noparatana rajdhani mahasathan, amorn piman avatarn satit, sakkatultiya visanukarn prasit.

BRUNEI
Capital: Bandar Seri Begawan
Area: 2,226 sq miles (5,765 sq km)
Population: 411,000
Languages: Malay, English
Religion: Moslem

CAMBODIA
Capital: Phnom Penh
Area: 69,898 sq miles (181,035 sq km)
Population: 8,543,000
Language: Khmer
Religion: Buddhist

INDONESIA
Capital: Jakarta
Area: 752,410 sq miles (1,948,732 sq km)
Population: 195,300,000
Language: Indonesian
Religion: Moslem

LAOS
Capital: Viangchan
Area: 91,429 sq miles (236,800 sq km)
Population: 4,158,000
Languages: Lao, French
Religion: Buddhist

MALAYSIA
Capital: Kuala Lumpur
Area: 129,251 sq miles (334,758 sq km)
Population: 18,200,000
Languages: Malay, English, Chinese
Religions: Moslem, Buddhist

PAPUA NEW GUINEA
Capital: Port Moresby
Area: 178,704 sq miles (462,840 sq km)
Population: 3,960,000
Languages: English, numerous others
Religion: Christian

PHILIPPINES
Capital: Manila
Area: 115,831 sq miles (300,000 sq km)
Population: 62,380,000
Languages: Pilipino, English, Spanish
Religions: Christian, Moslem

SINGAPORE
Capital: Singapore City
Area: 246 sq miles (636 sq km)
Population: 3,062,000
Languages: Malay, Chinese, English
Religions: Taoist, Buddhist

THAILAND
Capital: Bangkok
Area: 198,115 sq miles (513,115 sq km)
Population: 57,200,000
Language: Thai
Religion: Buddhist

VIETNAM
Capital: Hanoi
Area: 128,066 sq miles (331,689 sq km)
Population: 68,310,000
Languages: Vietnamese, French, Chinese
Religion: Buddhist

SINGAPORE

Singapore is a small island, just 25 miles (40 km) long by 15.5 miles (25 km) wide. It is an independent nation and one of the world's most important ports and trading centers. Many different races live in Singapore. Three-quarters of the population are Chinese, with smaller numbers of Malays and Indians. The remainder are Europeans, Arabs, or Japanese. These people all celebrate different festivals, making Singapore a lively and colorful place throughout the year.

Standard Chartered Bank

Clifford Pier

The Padang

Parliament

TAIWAN

PACIFIC OCEAN

Rice terrraces

MANILA

LUZON

PHILIPPINES

Sugarcane

Cebu

PHILIPPINES

Coral reefs

MINDANAO

Monkey-eating eagle

Zamboanga

Davao

Vinta boat

Coral reefs

CELEBES SEA

Coconuts

Sago palms

MOLUCCAS

Oil

Oil

Shrimps

Nutmeg

SERAM SEA

SERAM

Sago palms

Tuna

Spirit house

Coconuts

Jayapura

IRIAN JAYA

Tree kangaroo

△ Puncak Jaya 16,503 ft

Toraja house

CELEBES

Cloves

Coffee

Ujungpandang

BANDA SEA

Crabs

Irian Jaya native

Bird of paradise

Asmat warriors

PAPUA NEW GUINEA

△ MT. WILHELM 14,793 ft

PAPUA

NEW BRITAIN

Dancer and drum

PORT MORESBY

ONESIA

Komodo dragon

FLORES

Corn

TIMOR

SUMBA

Kupang

ARAFURA SEA

TIMOR SEA

AUSTRALIA

PAPUA NEW GUINEA

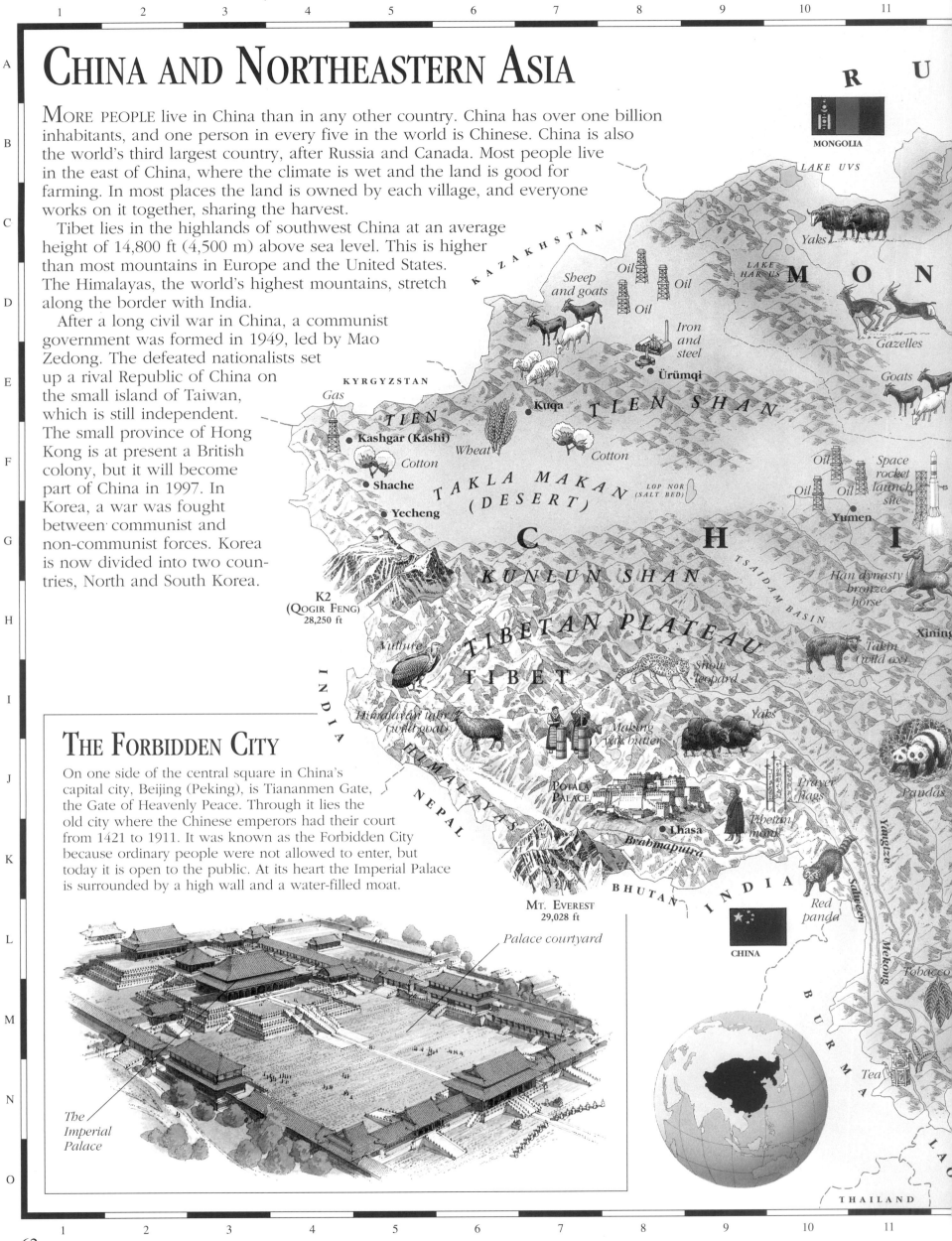

CHINA AND NORTHEASTERN ASIA

MORE PEOPLE live in China than in any other country. China has over one billion inhabitants, and one person in every five in the world is Chinese. China is also the world's third largest country, after Russia and Canada. Most people live in the east of China, where the climate is wet and the land is good for farming. In most places the land is owned by each village, and everyone works on it together, sharing the harvest.

Tibet lies in the highlands of southwest China at an average height of 14,800 ft (4,500 m) above sea level. This is higher than most mountains in Europe and the United States. The Himalayas, the world's highest mountains, stretch along the border with India.

After a long civil war in China, a communist government was formed in 1949, led by Mao Zedong. The defeated nationalists set up a rival Republic of China on the small island of Taiwan, which is still independent. The small province of Hong Kong is at present a British colony, but it will become part of China in 1997. In Korea, a war was fought between communist and non-communist forces. Korea is now divided into two countries, North and South Korea.

THE FORBIDDEN CITY

On one side of the central square in China's capital city, Beijing (Peking), is Tiananmen Gate, the Gate of Heavenly Peace. Through it lies the old city where the Chinese emperors had their court from 1421 to 1911. It was known as the Forbidden City because ordinary people were not allowed to enter, but today it is open to the public. At its heart the Imperial Palace is surrounded by a high wall and a water-filled moat.

Palace courtyard

The Imperial Palace

MONGOLIA

LAKE UVS

Yaks

LAKE HAR US

R U

M O N

Gazelles

Goats

KAZAKHSTAN

Sheep and goats

Oil

Oil

Oil

Iron and steel

Ürümqi

KYRGYZSTAN

Gas

TIEN

Kashgar (Kashi)

Kuqa

TIEN SHAN

Wheat

Cotton

Cotton

Oil

Oil

Oil

Oil

Space rocket launch site

Cotton

Shache

TAKLA MAKAN (DESERT)

LOP NOR (SALT BED)

Yumen

Yecheng

C H I

K2 (QOGIR FENG) 28,250 ft

KUNLUN SHAN

TSAIDAM BASIN

Han dynasty bronze horse

Vulture

TIBETAN PLATEAU

Takin (wild ox)

Xining

INDIA

TIBET

Snow leopard

Himalayan tahr (wild goat)

Making yak butter

Yaks

Pandas

HIMALAYAS

Potala Palace

Prayer flags

NEPAL

Tibetan monk

Yangtze

Lhasa

Brahmaputra

Salween

BHUTAN

INDIA

Red panda

CHINA

MT. EVEREST 29,028 ft

Mekong

Tobacco

BURMA

Tea

THAILAND

A
B
C
D
E
F
G
H
I
J
K
L
M
N
O

S S I A

S — 13 — 14 — 15 — 16 — 17 — 18 — 19 — 20 — 21 — 22 — 23

Sheep

ULAN BATOR

Gers (Mongol tents)

G O L I A

Cowboy and wild horse

G O B I   D E S E R T

Bactrian camels

I N N E R   M O N G O L I A

Goats

Locomotives

Iron and steel

Baotou

Sheep

N

GREAT WALL OF CHINA

Yinchuan

Wuwei

Cyclists

Millet

Cotton

Lanzhou

TERRACOTTA ARMY

Chemicals and textiles

Xi'an

Yams

Ducks

Luoyang   **Zhengzhou**

Porcelain

Yunxian

Wuhan

Iron and steel

Oil

Oil

Corn

Chengdu

Yangtze

Cotton

Rice

Millet

Chongqing

Chemicals and vehicles

Nanxian

Changsha

Tea

Yams

Guiyang

Limestone hills

Water buffalo plow

Guilin

Liuzhou

Sampan

Kunming

Guangzhou (Canton)

MACAU

Nanning

Sugarcane

Gibbon

VIETNAM

Malipo

Mengzi

Rubber trees

HAINAN

Kaoliang (cereal crop)

Coal

Songhua

Qiqihar

Vehicles

Coal

Oil

Harbin

Tiger

Oil

Soy beans

Vehicles

Changchun

Jilin

LAKE HULUN

TEMPLE OF HEAVEN

Wheat

Coal

Oil

Fushun

Shenyang

Anshan

Corn

Iron and steel

Liao

BEIJING (PEKING)

Dalian

Tianjin

Oil

Taiyuan

Jinan

Corn

Iron and steel

Qingdao

Fish

Wheat

Yellow River

Vehicles

Planting rice

Tobacco

Yangtze

Nanjing

Shanghai

Cotton

Hangzhou

Iron and steel

Junk

Nanchang

Wenzhou

Goldfish

Silk

Nanping

Ganzhou

Sugarcane

Planting rice

Pigs

Fuzhou

Shantou

Chaoyang

Skyscrapers of modern Hong Kong

HONG KONG

Shellfish

Junk fishing

NORTH KOREA

Diesel locomotives

P'YŎNGYANG

Electronics and vehicles

SEOUL

Shipbuilding

SOUTH KOREA

Fish

Shipbuilding

YELLOW SEA

Fish

NORTH KOREA

SOUTH KOREA

Shipbuilding

KOREA STRAIT

SEA OF JAPAN

EAST CHINA SEA

Fishing

T'AIPEI

TAIWAN

PHILIPPINE SEA

TAIWAN

SOUTH CHINA SEA

0   200   400   600   800 Kilometers

0   100   200   300   400   500 Miles

FACTS AND FIGURES

The Great Wall of China was built to protect the country's northern border against invaders. It is nearly 2,150 miles (3,460 km) long.

Longest river:
Yangtze (Chang Jiang), 3,915 miles (6,300 km).

Largest city population:
Shanghai (China), 9,300,000.

Gateway to the Chaotain Palace, one of many historic buildings in Nanjing, formerly the capital of China.

CHINA
Capital: Beijing (Peking)
Area: 3,689,631 sq miles (9,556,100 sq km)
Population: 1,181,580,000
Languages: Chinese
Religions: Confucianism, Buddhism, Taoism, Moslem
Currency: Yuan
Government: Communist republic

HONG KONG
Capital: Victoria
Area: 414 sq miles (1,072 sq km)
Population: 5,874,000
Languages: English and Chinese
Religions: Buddhism, Christianity, Taoism
Currency: Hong Kong dollar
Government: British colony

MACAU
Capital: Macau
Area: 7 sq miles (17 sq km)
Population: 448,000
Languages: Portuguese and Chinese
Religions: Buddhism, Christianity, Taoism
Currency: Pataca
Government: Portuguese colony

MONGOLIA
Capital: Ulan Bator
Area: 604,829 sq miles (1,566,500 sq km)
Population: 2,278,000
Language: Mongolian
Religions: Buddhism, Lamaism, Moslem
Currency: Tugrik
Government: Republic

NORTH KOREA
Capital: P'yŏngyang
Area: 46,540 sq miles (120,538 sq km)
Population: 22,250,000
Language: Korean
Religions: Buddhism, Confucianism, Taoism
Currency: Won
Government: Communist republic

SOUTH KOREA
Capital: Seoul
Area: 38,230 sq miles (99,016 sq km)
Population: 43,305,000
Language: Korean
Religions: Buddhism, Christianity, Confucianism
Currency: Won
Government: Republic

TAIWAN
Capital: T'aipei
Area: 13,900 sq miles (36,002 sq km)
Population: 20,785,000
Language: Chinese
Religions: Buddhism, Taoism, Christianity
Currency: New Taiwan dollar
Government: Republic

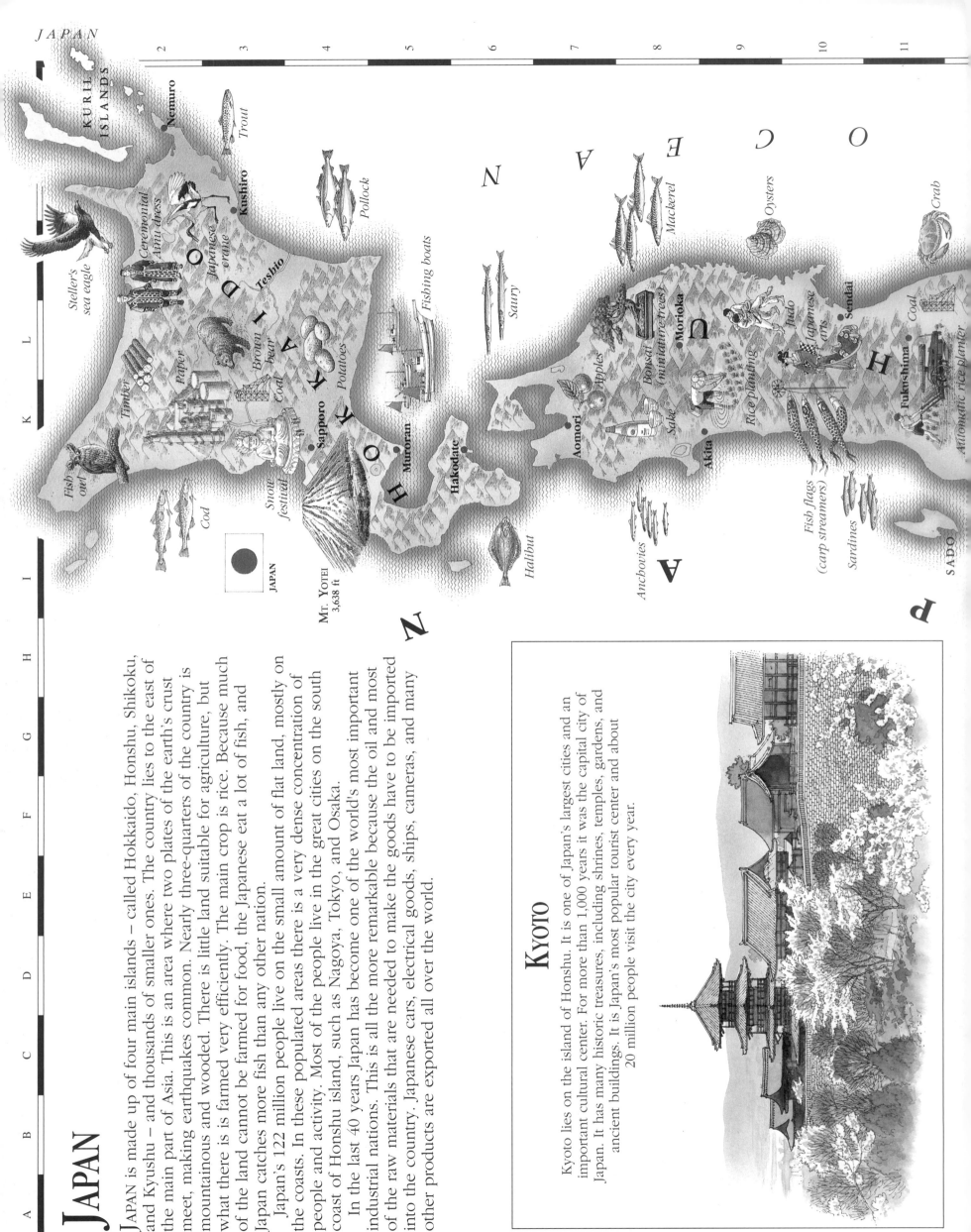

JAPAN

JAPAN is made up of four main islands – called Hokkaido, Honshu, Shikoku, and Kyushu – and thousands of smaller ones. The country lies to the east of the main part of Asia. This is an area where two plates of the earth's crust meet, making earthquakes common. Nearly three-quarters of the country is mountainous and wooded. There is little land suitable for agriculture, but what there is is farmed very efficiently. The main crop is rice. Because much of the land cannot be farmed for food, the Japanese eat a lot of fish, and Japan catches more fish than any other nation.

Japan's 122 million people live on the small amount of flat land, mostly on the coasts. In these populated areas there is a very dense concentration of people and activity. Most of the people live in the great cities on the south coast of Honshu island, such as Nagoya, Tokyo, and Osaka.

In the last 40 years Japan has become one of the world's most important industrial nations. This is all the more remarkable because the oil and most of the raw materials that are needed to make the goods have to be imported into the country. Japanese cars, electrical goods, ships, cameras, and many other products are exported all over the world.

KYOTO

Kyoto lies on the island of Honshu. It is one of Japan's largest cities and an important cultural center. For more than 1,000 years it was the capital city of Japan. It has many historic treasures, including shrines, temples, gardens, and ancient buildings. It is Japan's most popular tourist center and about 20 million people visit the city every year.

Steller's sea eagle

Fish owl

Timber

Paper

Ceremonial Ainu dress

Japanese crane

Brown bear

Coal

Potatoes

Snow festival

HOKKAIDO

Sapporo

Muroran

Hakodate

Mt. Yotei 3,638 ft

JAPAN

Cod

Nemuro

Trout

Kushiro

Pollock

Teshio

Fishing boats

Halibut

Saury

Mackerel

Oysters

Crab

Aomori

Apple

Sake

Bonsai (miniature trees)

Morioka

Judo

Japanese arts

Rice planting

Akita

Sendai

Coal

Fukushima

Automatic rice planter

HONSHU

Anchovies

Fish flags (carp streamers)

Sardines

SADO

KURIL ISLANDS

PACIFIC OCEAN

Tokyo, Japan's capital, and a major industrial port.

J A P A N
Capital: Tokyo
Area: 145,870 sq miles (377,801 sq km)
Population: 124,270,000
Language: Japanese
Religions: Shintoism, Buddhism
Currency: Yen

Temple statue at Nikko, Honshu.

FACTS AND FIGURES

Four largest islands: Honshu, Hokkaido, Kyushu, Shikoku. There are also about 4,000 small islands.

Highest mountain: Mt Fuji, 12,388 ft (3,776 m).

Main ports: Tokyo, Yokohama, Osaka, and Kobe.

Wettest area: All of Japan has high rainfall, but the wettest place is the southernmost island of Kyushu, where average rainfall reaches over 86.6 in (2,200 mm) per year.

Coldest area: Hokkaido has average winter temperatures of 14°F (-10°C).

Longest railway tunnel in the world: The Seikan Rail Tunnel in Japan runs for 33.46 miles (53.85 km) between Tappi Saki on Honshu island and Fukushima on Hokkaido.

World's largest fishing fleet: Japan catches around 14 percent of the total world catch – more than any other country. Each Japanese person eats an average of 65 lbs (30 kg) of fish a year.

World's tallest lighthouse: The steel lighthouse in Yokohama, Japan is 348 ft (106 m) high. It can be seen from 20 miles (32 km) away.

Food: Only 15 percent of the land, mostly on the coastal plains, can be farmed. But despite this, Japan is 70 percent self-sufficient in food.

World's top oil importer: Japan. The *Seawise Giant*, a Japanese tanker built in 1981, is the largest tanker in the world. It is almost 547 yards (500 m) long and can carry 622,630 U.S. tons of crude oil.

Largest cities: Tokyo, 30,300,000; Osaka, 16,900,000; Nagoya, 4,800,000; Yokohama, 3,220,350; Sapporo, 1,900,000; Fukuoka, 1,750,000; Kobe, 1,477,423; Kyoto, 1,461,140.

A typical Japanese garden in Hiroshima.

Skyscrapers of modern Tokyo

Tuna

Electronics

BRONZE BUDDHA (KAMAKURA)

IZU ISLANDS

Hitachi

Macaque

TOKYO

Electronics

Kawasaki Yokohama

Skiing

Shizuoka

Tea terraces

Cherry blossom

Nagano

Mt. Fuji 12,388 ft

Toyama

Serow

Cars

Nagoya

Pearls

Sumo wrestler

NAGOYA CASTLE

Bullet train

Fukui

Kyoto

Osaka

Terraced rice fields

GOLD PAVILION

Iron and steel

Kobe

Shipbuilding

Citrus fruits

Sardines

Fishing boats

Squid

Tottori

Shinto dignitary

Okayama

Satsumas

Crab

Oil tanker

Squid

OKI ISLANDS

SHIKOKU

Kochi

Loggerhead turtle

Shrimps

Shinto shrine

Torii gate

Hiroshima

MATSUYAMA CASTLE

Tofu (bean curd)

Miyazaki

Kabuki theatre

Iron and steel

Chemicals

Kumamoto

Rice planting

Sweet potatoes

Mackerel

KYUSHU

Octopus

OSUMI ISLANDS

Anchovies

Kitakyushu

Fukuoka

Pottery

Nagasaki

GOTO ISLANDS

Shellfish

Kagoshima

IKI ISLAND

TSU ISLAND

JAPAN

SEA OF JAPAN

EAST CHINA SEA

200 Kilometers
150
100
50
0

125 Miles
100
75
50
25
0

AFRICA

The Muhammad Ali mosque in Cairo, Egypt.

AFRICA, the world's second largest continent, is the warmest of all the continents. The only permanent snow and ice are found on the peaks of the highest mountains, such as Mount Kenya and Mount Kilimanjaro. In the regions near the centre of the continent, the hot and wet climate supports the dense jungle vegetation of the tropical rain forest. Today much of the forest has been cleared for farming and timber.

Moving away from the central regions, the climate becomes increasingly dry, and the forest gives way to tropical grassland, called savannah. For thousands of years the savannah has supported huge herds of plant-eating animals – gazelles, wildebeest, zebras, elephants, and giraffes – along with the predators who hunt and feed on them – lions, leopards, and hyenas. Today farming has greatly reduced the size of the herds, and some animals, such as the African elephant, are in danger of being wiped out forever.

Still farther to the north and south lie the great deserts, where the climate is so dry that few plants and animals can survive. Northern Africa is dominated by the Sahara, the world's largest desert. In the south lie the Kalahari and Namib deserts.

Africa is an immense plateau, broken by a few mountain ranges. In some areas a narrow coastal plain stretches along the edge of the plateau. Cutting across East Africa is the Great Rift Valley, with its many lakes and volcanoes. This long valley was formed centuries ago when land slipped down between huge cracks in the earth's crust. Some scientists believe that the land east of the Great Rift Valley will eventually break away from Africa and become a new continent, just as the Red Sea marks the place where Arabia once split away from the rest of Africa.

Off the east coast of Africa lies the island of Madagascar, which broke away from Africa over 50 million years ago. Because of the island's isolation, unique plants and animals have evolved there. Twenty species of lemur, an animal distantly related to the monkey, are only found there.

Open cast mining in South Africa.

Equatorial vegetation in Cameroon.

FACTS ABOUT AFRICA

Area: 11,712,434 sq miles (30,335,000 sq km).

Population: 613,566,000.

Number of independent countries: 47 (the most on any continent).

Largest countries: Sudan, 967,500 sq miles (2,505,813 sq km); Algeria, 919,595 sq miles (2,381,741 sq km).

Most populated countries: Nigeria, 124,300,000; Egypt, 55,105,000; Ethiopia, 54,040,000.

Largest cities: Cairo (Egypt), 9,300,000; Alexandria (Egypt), 3,350,000; Kinshasa (Zaire), 3,000,000.

Highest mountains: Mt. Kilimanjaro (Tanzania), 19,340 ft (5,895 m); Mt. Kenya (Kenya), 17,058 ft (5,199 m); Mt. Margherita (Uganda-Zaire), 16,763 ft (5,109 m); Ras Dashen Mtn. (Ethiopia), 15,158 ft (4,620 m).

Longest rivers: Nile, 4,145 miles (6,670 km), the longest in the world; Congo, 2,900 miles (4,667 km); Niger, 2,600 miles (4,184 km); Zambezi, 1,700 miles (2,735 km).

Largest lakes: Lake Victoria, 26,800 sq miles (69,400 sq km); Lake Tanganyika, 12,102 sq miles (32,900 sq km); Lake Nyasa, 11,100 sq miles (28,750 sq km); Lake Chad, area varies from 4,000-10,000 sq miles (10,000-26,000) sq km, according to the seasons.

Main deserts: Sahara (the largest in the world), about 3,474,927 miles (9,000,000 sq km); Kalahari, about 200,000 sq miles (517,998 sq km).

Largest islands: Madagascar, 226,658 sq miles (587,041 sq km); Réunion, 969 sq miles (2,510 sq km).

World's highest sand dunes: Dunes in the Sahara Desert can be up to 3 miles (5 km) long and 1,410 ft (430 m) high.

World's highest temperature: In 1922 the temperature in Al'Azizya (Libya) reached 136.4°F (58°C) in the shade.

World's largest man-made lake: Lake Volta (Ghana), which was formed by the Akosombo Dam, has a surface area of 3,275 miles (8,482 sq km).

Map labels: MEDITERRANEAN SEA, MOROCCO, TUNISIA, WESTERN SAHARA, ALGERIA, LIBYA, EGYPT, MAURITANIA, MALI, NIGER, CHAD, SUDAN, ERITREA, SENEGAL, GAMBIA, GUINEA BISSAU, GUINEA, BURKINA FASO, BENIN, NIGERIA, DJIBOUTI, SIERRA LEONE, IVORY COAST, GHANA, TOGO, CAMEROON, CENTRAL AFRICAN REPUBLIC, ETHIOPIA, SOMALIA, LIBERIA, SAO TOME & PRINCIPE, EQUATORIAL GUINEA, GABON, CONGO, ZAIRE, UGANDA, KENYA, RWANDA, BURUNDI, TANZANIA, ATLANTIC OCEAN, ANGOLA, ZAMBIA, MALAWI, MOZAMBIQUE, MADAGASCAR, INDIAN OCEAN, ZIMBABWE, NAMIBIA, BOTSWANA, SWAZILAND, SOUTH AFRICA, LESOTHO, SOUTH AMERICA

A
B
C
D

L
M
N
O

EUROPE

ASIA

A T L A N T I C

STRAIT OF GIBRALTAR

MEDITERRANEAN SEA

GULF OF SIRTE

MADEIRA

CANARY
ISLANDS

ATLAS MTS

**JEBEL
TOUBKAL
13,665 ft**

S A H A R A

*AHAGGAR
MTS*

*AIR
MASSIF*

*TIBESTI
MASSIF*

LAKE
NASSER

*NUBIAN
DESERT*

*ARABIAN
PENINSULA*

RED SEA

*ARABIAN
SEA*

CAPE
VERDE
ISLANDS

Senegal

Gambia

Niger

LAKE
CHAD

Nile

Nile

Atbara

Blue Nile

**RAS DASHEN MTN.
15,158 ft**

GULF OF ADEN

SOCOTRA

S A H E L

Benue

LAKE
VOLTA

Niger

*GULF OF
GUINEA*

BIOKO

△ **MT. CAMEROON
13,451 ft**

PRINCIPE·
SÃO TOMÉ

Congo

White Nile

LAKE
TURKANA

GREAT RIFT VALLEY

△ **MT. KENYA
17,058 ft**

MT. MARGHERITA △
16,763 ft

LAKE
MAI-NDOMBE

LAKE
VICTORIA

△ **MT. KILIMANJARO
19,340 ft**

SEYCHELLES

Congo

Ubangi

LAKE
TANGANYIKA

ZANZIBAR

ASCENSION

GREAT RIFT VALLEY

LAKE
NYASA

COMOROS

Zambezi

LAKE
KARIBA

ST HELENA

Okavango

Limpopo

*MOZAMBIQUE
CHANNEL*

MADAGASCAR

MAURITIUS
RÉUNION

NAMIB DESERT

*KALAHARI
DESERT*

Orange

DRAKENSBERG

I N D I A N

TRISTAN DA
CUNHA

CAPE OF
GOOD HOPE

O C E A N

O C E A N

NORTHERN AFRICA

DOMINATING NORTHERN AFRICA is the huge expanse of the Sahara Desert. The climate is wetter along parts of the north coasts, and here citrus fruits, grapes, and dates are grown. Along the Mediterranean coastline tourism is increasingly important. The largest countries in Northern Africa are Egypt and Sudan, both farming countries, and Libya and Algeria, which have rich supplies of oil and natural gas.

The few people who live in the Sahara Desert are mostly nomads, who move from place to place with their sheep and camels. Along the southern edge of the Sahara is an area of semi-desert called the Sahel, which stretches across the countries of Mauritania, Mali, Burkina Faso, Niger, and Chad. These are among the world's poorest countries. In recent years the people there have suffered terrible famines.

West Africa, which includes the countries of Nigeria, Ghana, Benin and Ivory Coast, is a fertile region in which such crops as coffee, peanuts, and cocoa are grown.

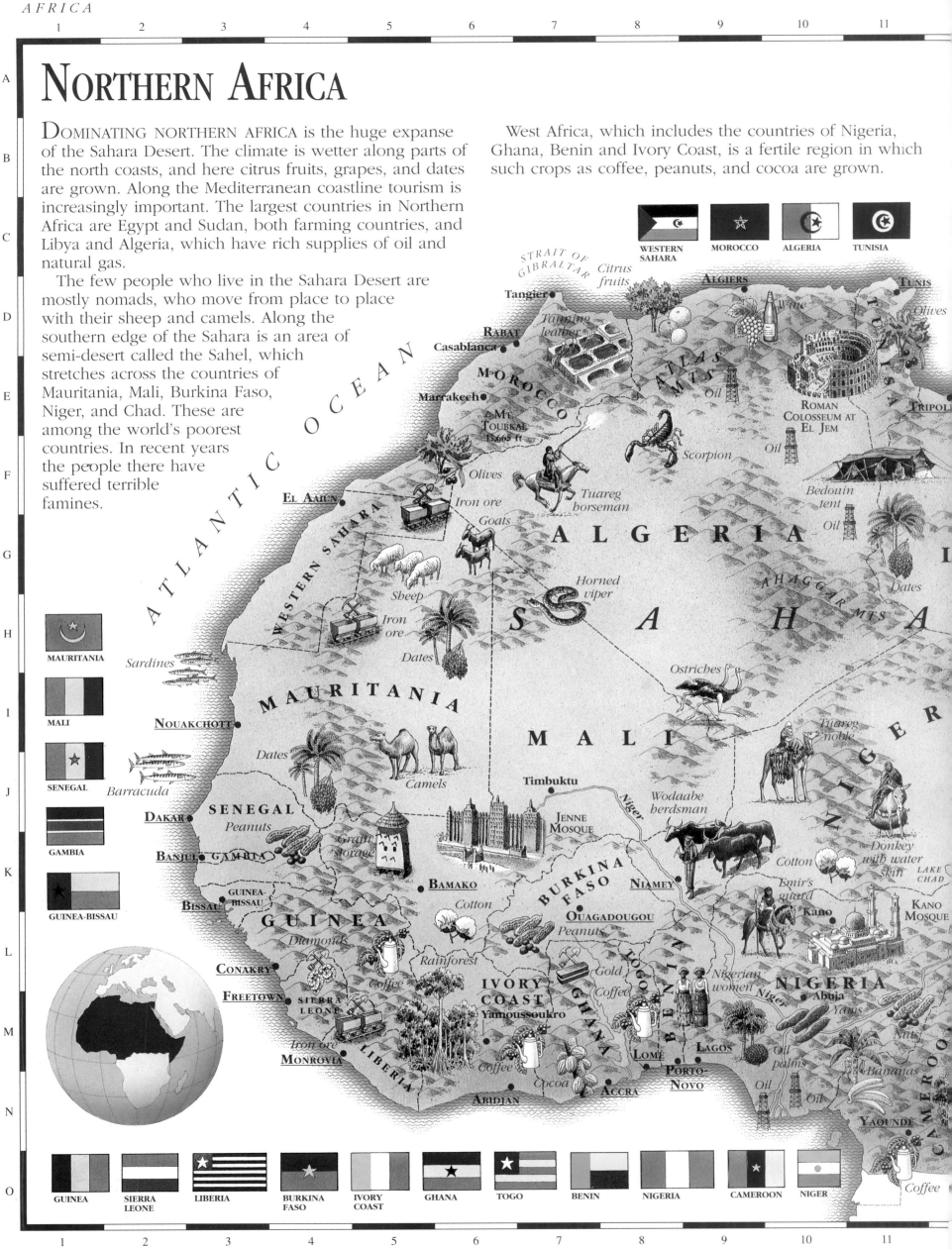

WESTERN SAHARA   MOROCCO   ALGERIA   TUNISIA

MAURITANIA

MALI

SENEGAL

GAMBIA

GUINEA-BISSAU

GUINEA   SIERRA LEONE   LIBERIA   BURKINA FASO   IVORY COAST   GHANA   TOGO   BENIN   NIGERIA   CAMEROON   NIGER

THE PYRAMIDS AND SPHINX

The pyramids of ancient Egypt were built in about 2500 B.C. to contain the mummified bodies of pharaohs, or kings. The three largest are at Giza. The Great Pyramid contains more than two million stone blocks. The Sphinx was probably built to guard the Pharaoh Chephren's body.

Pyramid of Chephren

Great Pyramid of Cheops

Pyramid of Mycerinus

FACTS AND FIGURES

Port Said lies at the entrance to the Suez Canal, which links the Mediterranean and Red Seas.

Longest river: Nile, 4,145 miles (6,670 km).

Highest mountain: Ras Dashen Mtn. (Ethiopia), 15,158 ft (4,620 m).

Largest lake: Lake Chad, area varies from 4,000–10,000 sq miles (10,000–26,000 sq km) according to the season.

ALGERIA
Capital: Algiers

BENIN
Capital: Porto-Novo, Cotonou

BURKINA FASO
Capital: Ouagadougou

CAMEROON
Capital: Yaoundé

CENTRAL AFRICAN REPUBLIC
Capital: Bangui

CHAD
Capital: N'Djamena

DJIBOUTI
Capital: Djibouti

EGYPT
Capital: Cairo

ERITREA
Capital: Asmera

ETHIOPIA
Capital: Addis Ababa

GAMBIA
Capital: Banjul

GHANA
Capital: Accra

GUINEA
Capital: Conakry

GUINEA-BISSAU
Capital: Bissau

IVORY COAST
Capital: Abidjan

LIBERIA
Capital: Monrovia

LIBYA
Capital: Tripoli

MALI
Capital: Bamako

MAURITANIA
Capital: Nouakchott

MOROCCO
Capital: Rabat

NIGER
Capital: Niamey

NIGERIA
Capital: Lagos

SENEGAL
Capital: Dakar

SIERRA LEONE
Capital: Freetown

SOMALIA
Capital: Mogadishu

SUDAN
Capital: Khartoum

TOGO
Capital: Lomé

TUNISIA
Capital: Tunis

WESTERN SAHARA
Capital: El Aaiún

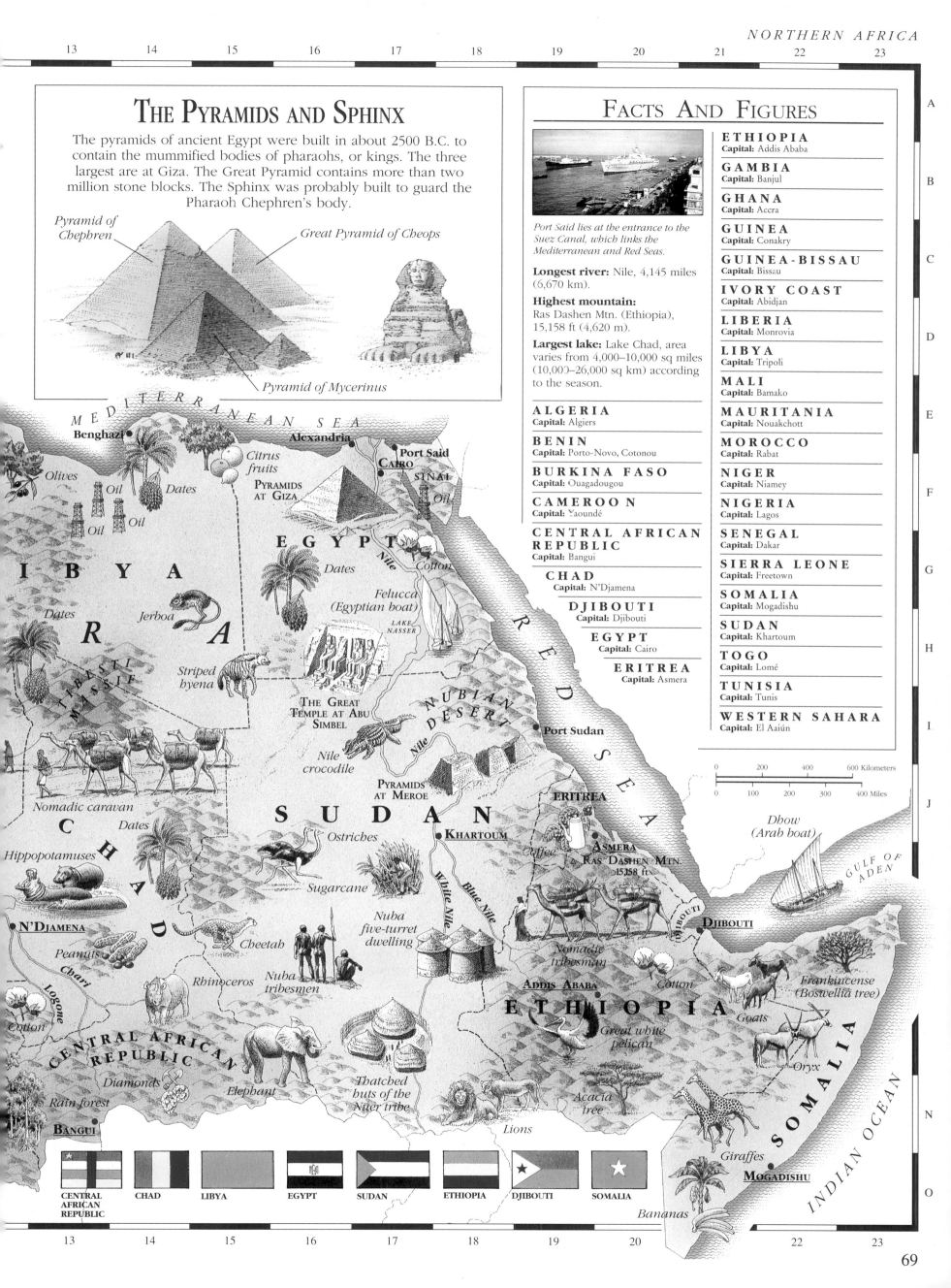

MEDITERRANEAN SEA

Benghazi
Alexandria
Port Said
CAIRO
SINAI
Oil

Olives
Oil
Oil
Oil
Dates
Citrus fruits
PYRAMIDS AT GIZA

LIBYA

EGYPT

Dates
Nile
Cotton

Dates
Jerboa

Felucca (Egyptian boat)

LAKE NASSER

Striped hyena

THE GREAT TEMPLE AT ABU SIMBEL

SAHARA

TIBESTI MASSIF

Nile crocodile

NUBIAN DESERT

RED SEA

Port Sudan

Nomadic caravan

Dates

PYRAMIDS AT MEROE

ERITREA

CHAD

SUDAN

ASMERA
RAS DASHEN MTN. 15,158 ft.

Dhow (Arab boat)

Hippopotamuses

Ostriches

KHARTOUM

White Nile

Blue Nile

Coffee

GULF OF ADEN

Sugarcane

Nuba five-turret dwelling

DJIBOUTI
DJIBOUTI

N'DJAMENA

Peanuts

Chari

Cheetah

Nuba tribesmen

Nomadic tribesman

Cotton

Rhinoceros

Nuba tribesmen

ADDIS ABABA

ETHIOPIA

Frankincense (Boswellia tree)

Logone

Cotton

Diamonds

Elephant

Thatched huts of the Nuer tribe

Great white pelican

Goats

Oryx

CENTRAL AFRICAN REPUBLIC

Rain forest

Acacia tree

Giraffes

SOMALIA

BANGUI

Lions

INDIAN OCEAN

MOGADISHU

Bananas

CENTRAL AFRICAN REPUBLIC | CHAD | LIBYA | EGYPT | SUDAN | ETHIOPIA | DJIBOUTI | SOMALIA

0 200 400 600 Kilometers
0 100 200 300 400 Miles

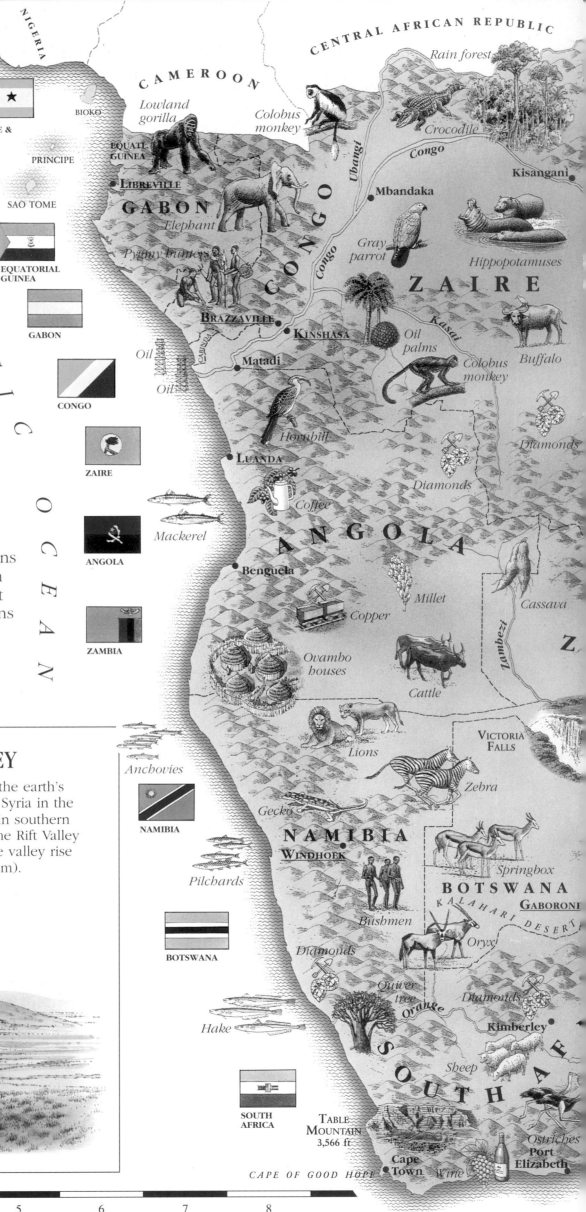

SOUTHERN AFRICA

SOUTHERN AFRICA contains a great variety of peoples and landscapes. In the northwest lies the rain forest of the Congo Basin. To the east lie the high grasslands of East Africa, where the peaks of Mt. Kenya and Mt. Kilimanjaro are snow-capped all year long and large herds of wild animals still roam the plains. The countries of Kenya, Uganda, and Tanzania contain rich farmland where coffee, tea, corn, and cotton are grown.

Angola, Zambia, and Zimbabwe are rich in diamonds, iron, and copper. Farther south lies the Kalahari Desert, which covers much of Botswana and Namibia. The world's richest diamond and gold mines are in South Africa. This country is also a major producer of fruit, wheat, cotton, and tobacco.

Much of southern Africa developed independently of the rest of the world. But from the late 1880s African culture was seriously disrupted when European nations took control of the region. Since 1959 Africans have regained their independence, except in South Africa where, in 1948, the government introduced a policy of apartheid (an Afrikaans word meaning "apartness"). This separated people according to their colour, and gave power to the white population only. Since 1990 apartheid has begun to crumble.

THE GREAT RIFT VALLEY

The Great Rift Valley is the largest crack in the earth's crust, stretching 5,400 miles (8,700 km) from Syria in the north, through the Red Sea to Mozambique in southern Africa. It is in East Africa that the scenery of the Rift Valley is most spectacular. In Kenya the walls of the valley rise almost straight up for 4,000 ft (1,250 m).

SAO TOME & PRINCIPE

EQUATORIAL GUINEA

GABON

CONGO

ZAIRE

ANGOLA

ZAMBIA

NAMIBIA

BOTSWANA

SOUTH AFRICA

SUDAN

ETHIOPIA

SOMALIA

Elephant

Coffee

Giant groundsel

UGANDA

KAMPALA

Cotton

LAKE TURKANA

Cheetah

KENYA

MT. KENYA 17,058 ft

NAIROBI

Coffee

Lions

KIGALI

LAKE VICTORIA

Wildebeest

Coconut palms

BUJUMBURA

BURUNDI

Gorilla

GREAT RIFT VALLEY

Masai herdsman

Dodoma

MT. KILIMANJARO 19,344 ft

Mombasa

Tourism

Dhow

TANZANIA

LAKE TANGANYIKA

Chimpanzee

GREAT RIFT VALLEY

Tea

Elephants

ZANZIBAR

DAR es SALAAM

Leopard

Copper

Rhinoceros

LAKE NYASA

Ndola

Crested hornbill

LILONGWE

Mangoes

Copper

Lusaka

KARIBA DAM

Nacala

LAKE KARIBA

Blantyre

Tea

ZIMBABWE

Bananas

HARARE

Soapstone carving

Plowshare tortoise

Lemur

Vanilla pods

Long-tailed ground roller

Bulawayo

GREAT ZIMBABWE

Beira

MOZAMBIQUE CHANNEL

ANTANANARIVO

MADAGASCAR

Baobab tree

Black lemur

Limpopo

Coelacanth

Cashew nuts

Gold

Giraffes

Chameleon

PRETORIA

Johannesburg

MAPUTO

Zulu

Octopus tree

MBABANE

SWAZILAND

Shrimps

MASERU

LESOTHO

Citrus fruits

Durban

Tourism

Umtata

Pineapples

Lobster

ALDABRA ISLANDS

COMOROS

MAYOTTE (Fr)

INDIAN OCEAN

Flags:
UGANDA
KENYA
RWANDA R
BURUNDI
TANZANIA
COMOROS
MALAWI
ZIMBABWE
MOZAMBIQUE
SWAZILAND
LESOTHO
MADAGASCAR

800 Kilometers
0 200 400 600

500 Miles
0 100 200 300 400

71

FACTS AND FIGURES

Zebra in the plains of Kenya. In recent years their numbers have been greatly reduced by hunting.

Highest mountains:
Mt. Kilimanjaro (Tanzania), 19,344 ft (5,896 m); Mt. Kenya (Kenya), 17,058 ft (5,199 m).

Longest rivers:
Congo, 2,900 miles (4,667 km); Zambezi, 1,700 miles (2,735 km).

Largest lakes: Lake Victoria, 26,800 sq miles (69,400 sq km); Lake Tanganyika, 13,860 sq miles (32,900 sq km).

Deepest lake: Lake Tanganyika, 4,708 ft (1,435 m).

Largest cities: Kinshasa (Zaire), 3,000,000; Cape Town (South Africa), 1,790,000.

ANGOLA
Capital: Luanda

BOTSWANA
Capital: Gaborone

BURUNDI
Capital: Bujumbura

COMOROS
Capital: Moroni

CONGO
Capital: Brazzaville

EQUATORIAL GUINEA
Capital: Malabo

GABON
Capital: Libreville

KENYA
Capital: Nairobi

LESOTHO
Capital: Maseru

MADAGASCAR
Capital: Antananarivo

MALAWI
Capital: Lilongwe

MOZAMBIQUE
Capital: Maputo

NAMIBIA
Capital: Windhoek

RWANDA
Capital: Kigali

SAO TOME & PRINCIPE
Capital: São Tomé

SOUTH AFRICA
Capitals: Pretoria, Cape Town

SWAZILAND
Capital: Mbabane

TANZANIA
Capital: Dar es Salaam

UGANDA
Capital: Kampala

ZAIRE
Capital: Kinshasa

ZAMBIA
Capital: Lusaka

ZIMBABWE
Capital: Harare

OCEANIA

OCEANIA IS THE SMALLEST of the continents and it has fewer people than any other continent except Antarctica. Oceania is sometimes called Australasia, after Australia, which is the only large piece of land it contains. The continent also includes the islands of New Guinea and New Zealand, and thousands of tiny islands scattered across the Pacific Ocean, many of which are too small to show on the map.

The city of Perth, Australia.

Australia, New Zealand and New Guinea were once joined to the other southern continents, but over millions of years they split off and drifted into the Pacific Ocean. Because Oceania is so isolated, many of the plants and animals which have evolved there are not found anywhere else in the world. The pouched mammals of Australia, such as the kangaroo, wallaby, and koala, and the flightless birds of New Zealand, such as the kiwi and the kakapo, are examples of this.

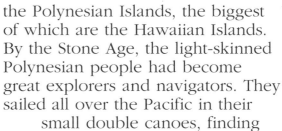

Maori carving, New Zealand.

The Pacific islands have been formed in a number of ways. Some of them are the tips of mountains or volcanoes which rise up from the ocean bed. Others are formed of coral, made up of the skeletons of millions of tiny sea creatures.

One of the Fijian islands.

The Pacific islands fall into three groups, depending on their position in the ocean. In the middle of the Pacific are the Polynesian Islands, the biggest of which are the Hawaiian Islands. By the Stone Age, the light-skinned Polynesian people had become great explorers and navigators. They sailed all over the Pacific in their small double canoes, finding their way from the position of the stars and the patterns of the waves. The Maori people of New Zealand are descended from Polynesians who settled there in about A.D. 900.

The Micronesian Islands are situated in the western Pacific. Like the Polynesians, the Micronesians were great seafarers, and traded throughout the region. The dark-skinned Melanesian people live on the islands closest to Australia and are related to the Australian Aborigines.

Today, tourism is an important industry in the Pacific islands, and this has brought many changes to the islanders' way of life.

Europeans first began to settle in Oceania in the 18th century. Most of the people who now live in Australia and New Zealand are descendants of settlers from the United Kingdom. More recently, immigrants have also come from other parts of Europe, Polynesia, and the Far East.

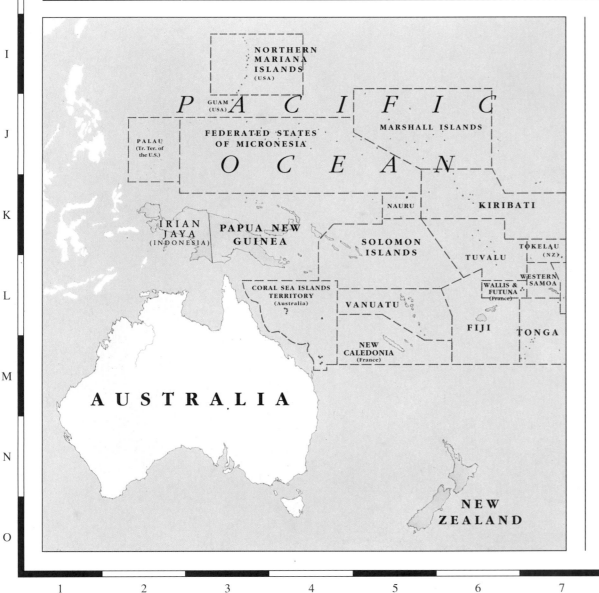

FACTS ABOUT OCEANIA

Area: 3,445,197 sq miles (8,923,000 sq km). Oceania is the smallest of the continents and covers only six percent of the world's land area.

Population: 25,800,000. Fewer people live in Oceania than any other continent, except Antarctica.

Number of independent countries: 13.

Largest country: Australia, 2,966,155 sq miles (7,682,300 sq km).

Most populated country: Australia, 17,420,000.

Largest cities: Sydney (Australia), 3,623,550; Melbourne (Australia), 3,039,100; Brisbane (Australia), 1,273,511; Perth (Australia), 1,158,387; Adelaide (Australia), 1,036,747; Auckland (New Zealand), 850,000.

Highest mountains: Mt. Wilhelm (Papua New Guinea), 14,793 ft (4,509 m); Mt. Cook (New Zealand), 12,349 ft (3,764 m); Mt. Kosciusko (Australia), 7,310 ft (2,228 m).

Longest river: Murray-Darling (Australia), 2,330 miles (3,750 km).

Largest deserts: Gibson Desert, Great Sandy Desert, Great Victoria Desert, Simpson Desert (all in Australia).

Largest islands: New Guinea, 312,168 sq miles (808,510 sq km); South Island, New Zealand, 58,080 sq miles (150,460 sq km).

Largest lakes: Lake Eyre (Australia), 3,700 sq miles (9,583 sq km); Lake Gairdner (Australia), 3,000 sq miles (7,770 sq km); Lake Torrens (Australia), 2,231 sq miles (5,780 sq km). Size varies according to the season. These are maximum areas.

Oldest rocks: The oldest rocks ever found on Earth are zircon crystals from the Jack Hills near Perth, Australia. They are 4.3 billion years old.

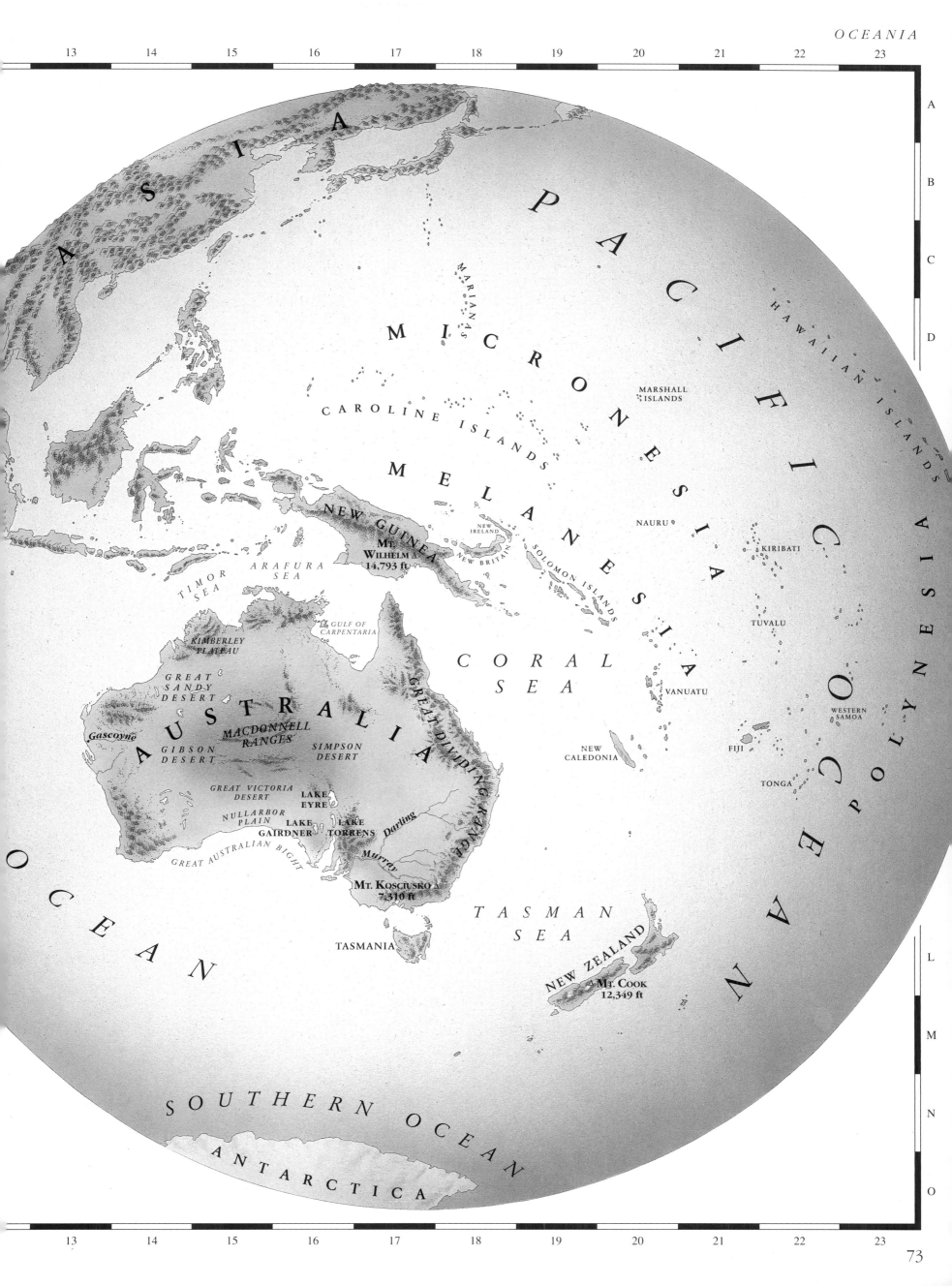

ASIA

PACIFIC

MICRONESIA

MELANESIA

POLYNESIA

HAWAIIAN ISLANDS

MARIANAS

CAROLINE ISLANDS

MARSHALL ISLANDS

NAURU

KIRIBATI

NEW GUINEA
Mt.
WILHELM▲
14,793 ft

NEW IRELAND

NEW BRITAIN

SOLOMON ISLANDS

TUVALU

ARAFURA SEA

TIMOR SEA

GULF OF CARPENTARIA

CORAL
SEA

VANUATU

WESTERN SAMOA

KIMBERLEY PLATEAU

GREAT SANDY DESERT

AUSTRALIA

GREAT DIVIDING RANGE

NEW CALEDONIA

FIJI

Gascoyne

MACDONNELL RANGES

GIBSON DESERT

SIMPSON DESERT

TONGA

GREAT VICTORIA DESERT

LAKE EYRE

NULLARBOR PLAIN

LAKE GAIRDNER

LAKE TORRENS

Darling

Murray

GREAT AUSTRALIAN BIGHT

Mt. KOSCIUSKO ▲
7,310 ft

TASMAN SEA

TASMANIA

NEW ZEALAND

▲ Mt. COOK
12,349 ft

OCEAN

PACIFIC

OCEAN

SOUTHERN OCEAN

ANTARCTICA

AUSTRALIA

AUSTRALIA is a country and a continent. It is almost as big as the United States. Much of the country is hot and dry, especially in the middle where there are deserts. Few people live in these dry areas, but there are large sheep and cattle farms called "stations" and some mining. East of the hills and mountains of the Great Dividing Range and on the island of Tasmania the climate is wetter, and it is here that most people live. Two-thirds of all Australians live in the small number of large cities, particularly the state capitals, such as Sydney, Melbourne, and Brisbane. The population of Australia is only 16 million people, compared with 245 million in the United States.

Millions of years ago, Australia drifted away from the other continents of the world. As a result, many of the plants and animals which have evolved there are not found anywhere else in the world. Many of the mammals, such as kangaroos and wombats, are marsupials that rear their young in pouches on their stomachs.

The first inhabitants of Australia were the Aborigines, who arrived about 40,000 years ago. Europeans did not settle in Australia until 200 years ago. Since 1945 the population has doubled, with people coming to Australia from many parts of the world.

THE GREAT BARRIER REEF

The Great Barrier Reef is a maze of about 2,500 coral reefs and islands stretching 1,200 miles (2,000 km) along the coast of Queensland. It contains over 300 species of coral and thousands of fish. Coral is formed by millions of tiny sea animals called polyps, which cement themselves together. The Great Barrier Reef is slowly being eaten away by creatures called crown-of-thorns starfishes. In order to protect the reef from further destruction by both humans and natural causes, the Great Barrier Reef Marine Park has been formed.

Darwin

Saltwater crocodile

Pearl oysters

Baobab tree

Diamonds

KING LEOPOLD RANGES

Broome

Sulphur-crested cockatoo

WOLF CREEK METEORITE CRATER

Termite nests

N O R T E R

GREAT SANDY DESERT

Port Hedland

A U S T

HAMERSLEY RANGE

LAKE MACKAY

Emu

LAKE DISAPPOINTMENT

THE OLGAS

Desert plant

Iron Ore

WESTERN

GIBSON DESERT

AYERS ROCK

MUSGRAVE

Gascoyne

Red Kangaroos

AUSTRALIA

Wild camels

S O U T

Grains

Hairy-nosed wombat

GREAT VICTORIA DESERT

Geraldton

Dingo

Gold

INDIAN-PACIFIC RAILWAY

Black swan

Kalgoorlie

NULLARBOR PLAIN

Perth
Fremantle

GREAT AUSTRALIAN

THE PINNACLES

Cattle

Sheep

Wine

Bottle-nosed dolphins

Albany

Sperm whale

Sailing

I N D I A N

INDIAN OCEAN

0 150 300 450 600 Kilometers
0 100 200 300 400 Miles

Aboriginal dance

GULF OF CARPENTARIA

GROOTE EYLANDT

Water buffalo

THERN TERRITORY

BARKLY TABLELAND

THE DEVIL'S MARBLES

Cattle

Mount Isa

RALIA

Alice Springs

Flying doctor

SIMPSON DESERT

RANGES

H AUSTRALIA

Opals LAKE EYRE

LAKE TORRENS

Woomera

LAKE GAIRDNER

Port Augusta

Whyalla

Iron and steel

IGHT

Shipbuilding

Great white shark

O C E A N

Rock lobster

Fairy penguins

BASS STRAIT

AUSTRALIA

Tasmanian devil

Apples *Hobart*

TASMA...

TORRES STRAIT

Aboriginal cave paintings

Coral reef

GREAT BARRIER REEF

Cattle

Sugarcane

Cairns

Road train

GREAT DIVIDING RANGE

Townsville

Coal

Mackay

Green turtle

Scuba diving

CORAL SEA

Coral reef

Coral reef

QUEENSLAND

Sheep

Sugarcane

Sheep

Wallabies

GREAT DIVIDING RANGE

Coal

Rockhampton

Grains

Sheep

Skyscrapers of modern Brisbane

Brisbane

Southport

NEW

Lyrebird

Sapphires

Pineapples

Pineapples

Koalas

River red gum tree

Darling

SOUTH

Broken Hill

Kookaburra

WALES

Coal

Tamworth

Bananas

Iron and steel

Windsurfing

Platypus

Paddle steamer

Cars

Adelaide

Mildura

Pelicans

Murrumbidgee

Wagga Wagga

Newcastle

Sydney

Wollongong

CANBERRA

SYDNEY OPERA HOUSE AND BRIDGE

Wine

Timber

VICTORIA

Murray

Albury

Bendigo

Ballarat

Melbourne

Geelong

Horse racing

AUSTRALIAN CAPITAL TERRITORY

Surfing

Skiing

Sharks

Sailing

TASMAN SEA

PORT ARTHUR PENAL SETTLEMENT

15 17 18 19 20 21 22 23

13 14 15 18 19 20 21 22 23

FACTS AND FIGURES

View of Sydney harbor, showing the bridge and the opera house.

Largest cities: Sydney, 3,623,500; Melbourne, 3,039,100; Brisbane, 1,273,511.

Longest river: Murray-Darling, 2,330 miles (3,750 km).

Largest lake: Lake Eyre (dry for part of the year), max. of 3,700 sq miles (9,583 sq km).

World's leading wool producer: Australia produces 25 percent of the world's wool. There are around 10 sheep per person in Australia.

World's longest fence: The dingo-proof fence around the main sheep-grazing areas in Queensland is made of wire mesh and is over 1,553 miles (2,500 km) long.

Koalas are only found in Australia and are a protected species.

AUSTRALIA
Capital: Canberra
Area: 2,966,155 sq miles (7,682,300 sq km)
Population: 17,420,000
Language: English
Religion: Christian
Currency: Australian dollar

STATES AND TERRITORIES:

NEW SOUTH WALES
State capital: Sydney
Area: 309,500 sq miles (801,600 sq km)
Population: 5,930,000

NORTHERN TERRITORY
Territory capital: Darwin
Area: 519,771 sq miles (1,346,200 sq km)
Population: 160,000

QUEENSLAND
State capital: Brisbane
Area: 666,876 sq miles (1,727,200 sq km)
Population: 2,981,000

SOUTH AUSTRALIA
State capital: Adelaide
Area: 379,925 sq miles (984,000 sq km)
Population: 1,465,000

TASMANIA
State capital: Hobart
Area: 26,178 sq miles (67,800 sq km)
Population: 463,000

VICTORIA
State capital: Melbourne
Area: 87,877 sq miles (227,600 sq km)
Population: 4,455,000

WESTERN AUSTRALIA
State capital: Perth
Area: 975,101 sq miles (2,525,500 sq km)
Population: 1,672,000

AUSTRALIAN CAPITAL TERRITORY
Territory capital: Canberra
Area: 927 sq miles (2,400 sq km)
Population: 294,000

NEW ZEALAND

NEW ZEALAND lies in the Pacific Ocean, about 1,000 miles (1,600 km) southeast of Australia. The country is made up of two main islands: the North Island and the South Island. Most people live on the North Island, which has a warm, tropical climate.

The first people to reach New Zealand were the Maoris, who started to settle there around AD 900. They sailed to New Zealand from the Polynesian islands in small, open boats. The first European to sight the country was the Dutch explorer, Abel Tasman, in 1642. New Zealand became a British colony in 1840 and an independent country in 1907.

Today the population is a mixture of Maoris and people of British descent. The country's wealth comes from industry and farming, particularly raising cattle and sheep. New Zealand is the world's biggest exporter of lamb and second largest exporter of dairy products.

HOT SPRINGS

In the region around Rotorua, on the North Island, hot water bubbles out of the ground. In some places there is such pressure underground that water is forced out in a jet called a geyser, reaching heights of up to 230 ft (70 m). The steam produced in this area is used to drive electric power stations.

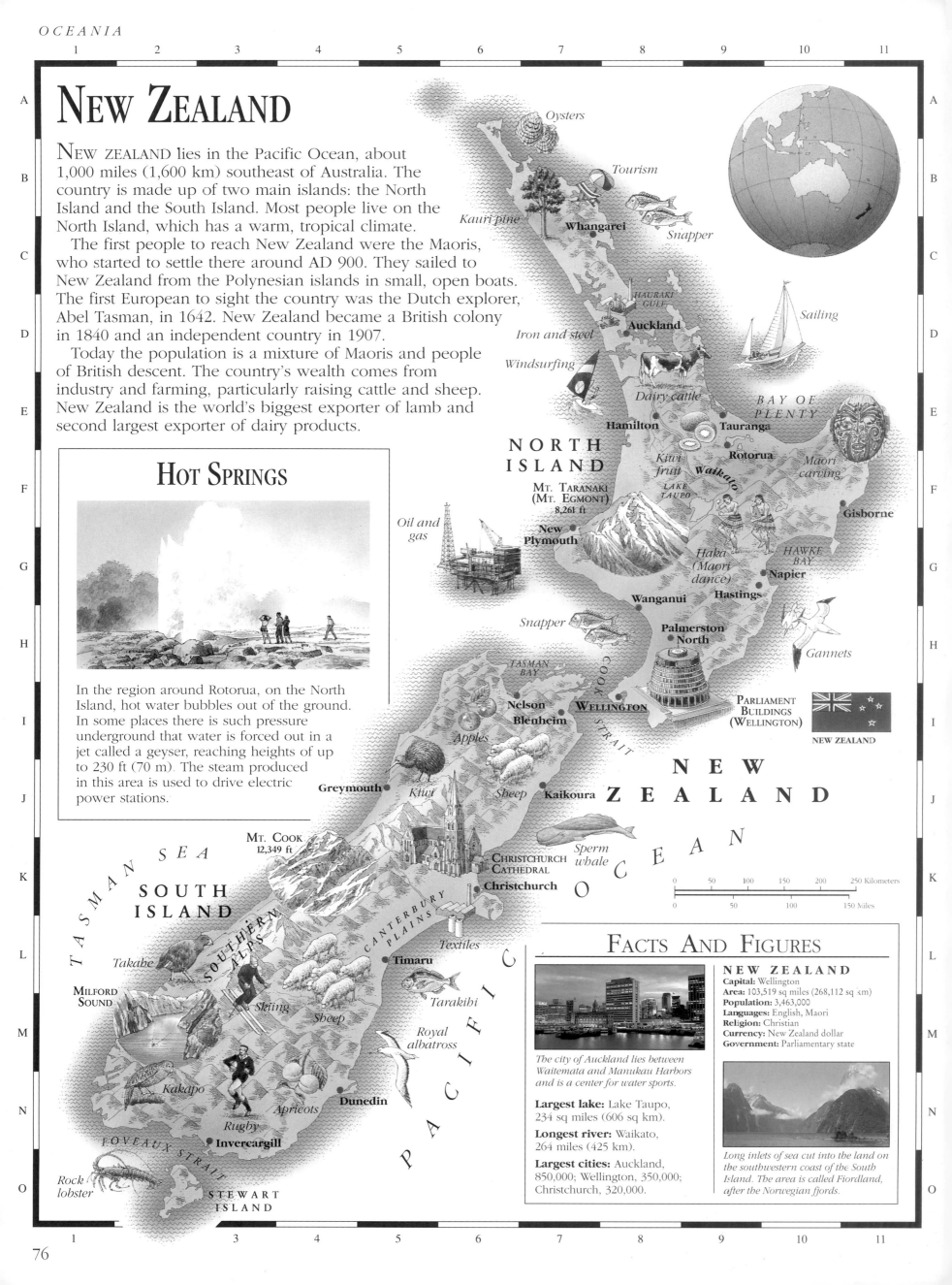

Map labels (North Island):
Oysters
Tourism
Kauri pine
Whangarei
Snapper
Sailing
HAURAKI GULF
Iron and steel
Auckland
Windsurfing
Dairy cattle
BAY OF PLENTY
Hamilton
Tauranga
NORTH ISLAND
Rotorua
Maori carving
Kiwi fruit
LAKE TAUPO
Waikato
MT. TARANAKI (MT. EGMONT) 8,261 ft
Haka (Maori dance)
Gisborne
Oil and gas
New Plymouth
HAWKE BAY
Napier
Snapper
Wanganui
Hastings
Palmerston North
Gannets
Parliament Buildings (Wellington)
NEW ZEALAND

Map labels (South Island):
TASMAN BAY
COOK STRAIT
WELLINGTON
NEW ZEALAND
Nelson
Blenheim
Apples
Kiwi
Sheep
Kaikoura
Sperm whale
Greymouth
MT. COOK 12,349 ft
CHRISTCHURCH CATHEDRAL
Christchurch
TASMAN SEA
SOUTH ISLAND
SOUTHERN ALPS
Takahe
Skiing
Sheep
CANTERBURY PLAINS
Textiles
Timaru
MILFORD SOUND
Tarakihi
Royal albatross
PACIFIC OCEAN
Kakapo
Apricots
Dunedin
Rugby
Invercargill
FOVEAUX STRAIT
Rock lobster
STEWART ISLAND

FACTS AND FIGURES

The city of Auckland lies between Waitemata and Manukau Harbors and is a center for water sports.

NEW ZEALAND
Capital: Wellington
Area: 103,519 sq miles (268,112 sq km)
Population: 3,463,000
Languages: English, Maori
Religion: Christian
Currency: New Zealand dollar
Government: Parliamentary state

Largest lake: Lake Taupo, 234 sq miles (606 sq km).

Longest river: Waikato, 264 miles (425 km).

Largest cities: Auckland, 850,000; Wellington, 350,000; Christchurch, 320,000.

Long inlets of sea cut into the land on the southwestern coast of the South Island. The area is called Fiordland, after the Norwegian fjords.

Scale:
0 50 100 150 200 250 Kilometers
0 50 100 150 Miles

INDEX

This index contains the names of places shown on continental and country maps. The page number is given in bold type after the place name. The grid reference follows in lighter type (see also page 13, How to Use This Atlas).

ACKNOWLEDGMENTS

Dorling Kindersley would like to thank the following:
Kate Woodward and Anna Kunst for research, Chris Scollen and Richard Czapnik for additional design help, and Struan Reid for editorial assistance.

Picture Research Cynthia Hole

Political Maps Luciano Corbella

Picture credits
(r = right, l = left, t = top, c = centre, b = bottom)

Australian Overseas Information Service, London 75tr, 75br
Australian Tourist Commission, London 72tr

de Beers 66tr
Charles Bowman 16br, 25tr, 34c, 51tl, 51tl, 59tr, 59br, 76tl,
Canadian High Commission 16tc, 19tc
Caribbean Tourist Office 27tr
The J. Allan Cash Photolibrary 6tr, 6bl, 12tl, 12br, 20tr, 23br, 23bl, 36tl, 36br, 45tl, 76br,
Lester Cheeseman 52bc, 65tl, 65tr, 65bc, 66tr
Chilean Embassy 33br, 33bl
Chinese Tourist Office 63br
Bruce Coleman Ltd / Fritz Prenzel 7cl,
Commission of the European Communities 34tl
Susan Cunningham 31br
Richard Czapnik 66c
Egyptian Tourist Office 57tr, 69tr

Chris Fairclough Colour Library 12c, 21tr, 43tr, 43br, 45c, 52tr, 72c, 72bl,
Fiat Press Office 46c
French Railways Ltd 39cr
Susan Griggs Agency / Rob Cousins 7tl; George Hall 12tr
Robert Harding Picture Library 6tl
Hutchison Library / John Downom 6br; Anwa Tully 12bl
The Image Bank / Guido Rossi 12bc
Italian State Tourist Office 46tl
Kenyan Tourist Office 71tr
Anna Kunst 55tr, 55cr
Keith Lye 16cl, 28tl, 28bc, 52tr, 57br, 63tr
Hugo Maertens 41br

Norwegian Tourist Office 14tr, 15tr
Peruvian Embassy 28tr, 31tr
Roger Priddy 34tr, 36tr, 39tr, 39br, 46cl
South American Pictures 33tl
Spanish National Tourist Office 49tr
The Telegraph Colour Library 41bl
Travel Photo International 7tr, 7cr, 41tr, 43cr, 45br, 49br
Zefa Picture Library 12cr
Zentrale Farbbild Agentur / D. Frobisch 7br

Every effort has been made to trace the copyright holders and we apologise in advance for any unintentional omissions. We would be pleased to insert the appropriate acknowledgment in any subsequent edition of this book.